Kind of Heart

By

Molly Lemmons

ISBN: 1-933582-35-9
1978933582359

Cover design by Jinger Heaston

POR: PawPrintsPOD

Printed in the United States of America

ACKNOWLEDGMENTS

It would be impossible to put together a book without the encouragement of friends and family. There are many who encouraged me, but I especially want to thank those who "went the extra mile" in helping me to believe in myself and stick to that belief:

Sally Clark
Linda Henley
Ed Koonce
Roger Lemmons

I also want to acknowledge the teacher of our youth group as we were growing up. He had a tremendous influence for good on the lives of my sister, Sally, and my brother, Bob, and me. Our two little sisters did not have the honor of sitting in his class as we did. They came along a little later. But I want him to know how very much he was appreciated then, and now. His name is:

LIONEL WALKER

Table of Contents

Introduction
Christmas Time Magic for Children

S entiments of the heart come into full focus only after you
reach a point in life to appreciate them. You reach that
point when things that happen around you begin to shift
your thoughts to memories of family, friends, and home.

Just recall the times when you were small and went to your
grandmother's house for Christmas: She had the tree loaded
with gifts, the table with food, and a fire glowing in the fireplace; when you went caroling with your cousins, and someone
invited you in for a cup of hot cocoa on a cold, snowy night; the
times you climbed out of that deep, downy feather bed with the
homemade ticking and peeked into the living room where you
saw the most beautiful tree in the world! Bare feet were cold on
the hardwood floor and the room was cold, too, because they
kept that part of the house shut off to save on heating costs.
But you didn't notice how you were shivering as you shuffled
through "a million gifts!"

The next day, the room would be warm from the fireplace,
and there would be two grandparents, their nine children and
their spouses, and 24 grandchildren, and your grandmother
would have made at least three gifts for each of them. That did
not even count all the gifts they exchanged with each other, so
in your mind, there really were a "million" gifts. You would sort
through all of them, find the ones with your name and stack
them neatly in a corner so that tomorrow whomever they chose
to be the "Elf" (to pass out the gifts) wouldn't make you wait so

long. The house of my grandmother and grandfather (we called them "Mama-Dear" and "Papa-Dear") was packed with people on Christmas Day, and the house rang with laughter and vibrated with love. Christmas at Mama-Dear and Papa-Dear's house was the best time of the year.

These are the kinds of memories that you come to appreciate as sentiments of the heart come full circle into your life. These memories were first published as a weekly newspaper column I wrote for the Mustang News (Mustang, Oklahoma). I called the column "Kind of Heart," because I write nostalgia, inspiration, and sometimes humor for kind-of-heart people. Bringing these columns together in a book, I hope to bring you fond remembrances of your own childhood, maybe even stir a gentle spirit within you that has lain dormant so long that you forgot you had it. With the stress of daily life, it is easy to forget where you've been, and unless you remember where you've been, you can't appreciate where you're going.

Now our nation seems to be struggling to get back to the basic values that made it great. I feel that it is both timely and appropriate to pause and reflect on where we have been. Maybe one of my memories will bring a smile or just brighten your day a little. But, whatever you glean from it, I hope you enjoy this collection of reflections from my heart to yours.

MAGNET MESSAGE:

Show us, O God, the purpose You intended for our lives and give us the courage to stand up for that purpose. In Jesus' Name, Amen.

"...whatsoever things are true, honest, just, pure, lovely...think on these things." Philippians 4:8

1. My Mother's Scrapbook

The loose pages were tattered around the edges, the clippings yellowed with time, but the beautiful penmanship still jumped off the pages in perfect clarity, the white ink in sharp contrast to the black pages.

The aging photos, black and white with fancy scrollwork around the edges, were a declaration of the era in which they had been taken. Lovingly and carefully mounted, time had not erased the beauty of the memories contained in my mother's scrapbook.

The lovely raven-haired young college girl who laughed back at me from the photographs gave me another insight into the beauty of Mother's girlhood days. As I turned each page, I met the man who was to be our father as the entire book told of their love and courtship.

Tall, skinny, and lanky, the dark and handsome man standing proudly beside his new car was the man our mother would marry. Sandwiched in between the pictures, little slips of paper were glued. On them Daddy had signed his name when he "checked out" his date from then-North Central State Teachers College in Denton, Texas, where Mother was attending college and living in the dormitory. Under every picture Mother had written an expression of the way she was feeling when she had so lovingly mounted them in her keepsake book.

She coined a word that she would one day tell us she made up by combining two words---rambunctious and fabulous---and she used them often to describe this young man in the picture beside her. Underneath one such picture, she wrote: "Look at him! Now isn't he just ramdulous?"

Her bubbly personality and happy disposition was all over every page as I read the one-liners in describing each picture. It was like reading her diary.

There was a picture of the two of them on a sitting on a rock wall that surrounded a city park. Mother has on a beautiful dress with a flutter-ruffle around the neck, a darling picture hat, and T-strap shoes with the spool heels. Daddy is sitting very close to her. It is a picture, that as a teenager, I would get a magnifying glass to get a closer look to see if they were holding hands. I was forever trying to find proof that Mother and Daddy acted differently than the way they taught us to act. I never could.

As big a talker as Mother was, there were private things of the heart that were kept just that way--private. If they held hands or kissed before they were married, I could never find it in pictures. She once told me during one of our talks about the proper dating behavior of a Christian girl, that she and Daddy did not kiss until they had dated a year.

Knowing that our parents did not set standards for us, which they themselves did not follow, was a wonderful example for us children and provided the security necessary to encourage us to do the same.

I turned a page and saw Mother in her back yard in a new "jump suit." It had wide, flared legs. It had splashes of flowers in the print, and Mother had taken a tad of cotton, dipped in

mercurochrome and tinted the flowers pink. She told me that her mother cautioned her not to show anyone the picture because it was "immodest."

Toward the end of the scrapbook, the pictures are of the two honeymooners at Turner Falls Park. There's Daredevil Daddy, sitting on the falls in a funny looking suit with a top, and Mother down below in the water. I thought again, of how fortunate we are to have had these two precious people in our lives. Every day I live, I am reminded more and more of this tremendous blessing, and with that thought, I closed My Mother's scrapbook.

MAGNET MESSAGE:

The old gentleman sat in his recliner reading a newspaper when his grandson approached his chair and asked, "Gramps, what did your generation wear for safe sex?"

The old gentleman, laying aside his paper, and removing his glasses, looked up at the young man and gently and quietly replied, "A wedding ring."

Dear Father, may we be a nation with morality and values, realizing that marriage is a sacred gift from You, through which the happiness and fulfillment You have ordained is found. When this is once again practiced, a blessed side effect just might be the eradication of the social diseases that plague our nation. In Jesus' name, Amen.

2. The Love Letters in the Attic

Once, when I was small, my cat had her kittens in the attic of the garage, and I climbed the ladder to try to find them. As I crawled along the floor to keep from bumping my head on the low ceiling, I was amazed at how much stuff was stored up there.

I wove myself between and behind so many boxes, I wondered if I would ever find the newborn kittens. Finally, at the very back, over in a dark corner, I heard the squirming little purr balls. After seeing for myself that they were all right, and acclimating them to my touch and voice so that they would not grow up wild, I began to crawl back out.

Over at the other end of the dark attic, tucked into a corner, was an old trunk that I had never before seen. Curiosity got the best of me, and I inched my way over to it. A stream of sunlight that had found its way through a crack in the garage wall gave me just enough light to survey its contents. Boy howdy! Had I found a treasure! My parents' love letters, exchanged when they were dating and after they became engaged! The letters were tied in neat little bundles, and I stuffed as many of them in pockets as I could. I planned to find a good light to read what I thought would be very interesting.

Once situated in the privacy of my closet, I settled myself down to read. I must have spent all day in that closet! Those letters were so wonderful I could hardly wait to get back out to the old trunk and get the rest of them. I could just visualize Mother writing the letters. They were filled with humor, love of

life, and love for Daddy. Her bubbly personality literally jumped off the pages, and her words made me smile. Her large hand-writing was open and broad. I could tell that she once had taught penmanship and English, too, as she expressed herself openly and honestly. I could chuckle at her sense of humor, but I could also be deeply moved at her profound capacity to love.

Daddy, on the other hand, communicated the depth of his love for Mother with poetic expressions that could measure up to any well-known poet of the day. Daddy had always enjoyed poetry, and every night, when we were small, he loved to have us all pile around him as he quoted his favorites to us:"Crossing the Bar," "Thanatopsis," "The Barefoot Boy," "The Spider and the Fly," and "The Psalm of Life." His love of poetry spilled over into all aspects of his life. He made something poetic of everything. These letters to Mother prove it, I thought. For him to describe Mother as a "rose among thorns," and "as bright and pure as the driven snow," was romantic and magical to me as I read these priceless masterpieces.

As I sat there alone in my closet, I wondered how this quiet, tall, dark, handsome man had ever had a chance to talk to the gig-gly, vivacious, talkative beauty he asked to marry him. Her letters were filled with chatter, humor, anticipation, while his were serious, filled with life's depth of meaning, plans for God's place in their home-to-be, and his love for her that would never die.

I kept the secret of the letters--for a while--but finally, temp-tation got the best of me and I decided to tell everybody. They made me feel happy, secure and safe, and I wanted to share them with anyone who might want to read them--for a fee!

One day when Mother was out shopping, I called in all of the neighborhood kids to come over to our garage. I lined them up and one by one, charged them five cents apiece to read a let-ter. By late afternoon, I pulled in quite a handsome profit.

Mother needed an explanation as to where I had gotten the

extra money, and I proudly announced, "All the kids loved the letters!" "What letters?" she asked. I excitedly told her of my discovery in the garage attic and for some reason, she did NOT share my enthusiasm, and I was in great trouble. I had crossed the line of respect and privacy, and I had greatly disappointed her.

The letters disappeared from the trunk, and all the beauty of Daddy's poetry seemed lost forever--that is, until one letter surfaced when Daddy retired and built them a house in Mustang, Oklahoma. During the moving process, one lone letter was found among papers in Daddy's filing cabinet. All five us asked for a copy for framing.

There would be no protests by then. We could all have a copy if we wanted it. The letter mentions to Mother, "Just think, Polly, maybe 40 years to spend together; on the other hand, two weeks seems a long time to have to wait to start that 40, maybe 50 years."Their mutual devotion, seasoned for 63 years, blended two lives and two hearts into one love---a love strong enough to cross the barrier of time, taking flight, and in immortality, merge forever into eternity!

And I was fortunate enough to get a "sneak peek" into the beginning of it all the day I found the Love Letters in the Attic.

MAGNET MESSAGE:

Thank You, God for the many years of married life You gave to my beloved parents. As the sorrows of life cross our paths, give us memories to sustain us to the day of Your coming. In Jesus' name, Amen.

"Keep your father's commandment, and forsake not your mother's teaching." Proverbs 6:20

3. *Wings of Angels*

The thunder claps--the lightning flashes! Two scared little girls huddle close and pull the covers over their heads.

"What color are your wings going to be?" one whispers to the other.

"Mine are going to be blue--shining with silver!"

"Mine are going to be pink--glittering with gold!"

The two little girls are selecting the colors for their heavenly wings.

"What do you think it will be like?" the little blue child asks her older sister.

"Lots of clouds, and lots of gold," the little pink child tells her little sister.

"I'm sorry if I was mean today," pink says to blue.

"That's okay, I started it," blue says to pink.

"Did I say 'I love you' today?"

"No."

"Well, I do."

"I do you, too."

"Did you say your prayer yet?"

"Yes, but maybe I better say it again!"

A large clap of thunder, the kind you hear and know lightning has struck something, causes the two little girls to scoot further down to the end of the bed and bury themselves under the heavy quilts.

"You okay?"

"Yes, but I am scared, Sister!" the blue one says

"It's okay," the older pink one answers, taking her little sister's hand.

The torrents of rain begin to pound the roof.

"Will our wings be fluffy?"

"Will they wilt in the rain?"

"I want mine to be lace, but will lace fly?"

The mother peeks into the room and sees two little lumps at the end of the bed under a pile of covers. She hears the sniffs of the younger sister, and the assurances of the older sister. She worries that they will smother under all of that cover, and as she is about to "dig them out," she hears her older daughter tell her younger daughter, "We better crawl out and check on Mother and Daddy. They may need someone to help them not be afraid."

The mother quietly returns to her room, and the lumps at the end of the bed begin to squirm.

As they wriggle their way back to the head of the bed, the rain begins to let up, and the lightning distances itself further and further away.

"Sister," the younger one whispers, "I think I'll wait on my wings a while longer."

"I believe I will, too" the older sister replies. "No sense rushing our order."

By now, all is quiet outside. The storm has passed. Inside

the cozy bedroom, two little girls have fallen safely asleep, confident that their pink and blue wings--on order-- will be held for them until a later time.

MAGNET MESSAGE:

Give us the faith of a small child as we try to live our lives in accordance to Your will. In Jesus' name, Amen.

"Whosoever shall humble himself as a little child,
the same is the greatest in the kingdom of Heaven." Matt. 18:4

4. The Magic of Gone With the Wind

I remember the first time I saw the movie, Gone With the Wind. It made a profound impression on my young mind, and although I was very small, there are certain scenes that I can vividly recall.

We were living in the same Texas town in which I had been born when the exciting news of the day broke. The long-awaited film was to open in nearby Dallas, and already the sale of tickets had escalated to a height unheard of during those years.

Our family left early in the morning that day to attend a matinee performance of the famous film. I had no earthly idea what a "picture show" was, but I was about to find out.

I probably remember as much about the theater as I remember about the movie! When I crawled up on the wooden seat, the bottom folded double, throwing my legs straight up. I clung to the handles to keep from sliding through the crack and, I thought, disappearing forever! I had to concentrate to remember to sit straight against the back of the seat with legs stuck out in front of me as I gripped the armrests.

It was during this deep concentration on trying to "tame" the theater seat that seemed determined to swallow me, that the movie began. The beauty of the sound track and the hooped and lacy Southern Belle gowns caught my fancy and mesmer-

ized me, but there were two scenes that have stayed forever stamped on my mind. Both of them involved Scarlet's horse.

The first one was the burning of Atlanta when the horse was led through and around it. I cried. I climbed onto Mother's lap and she hugged me. She thought I was afraid. I was not. I was worried about that horse. I just knew he would be burned up. I wanted to run up to the screen and help him. Mother explained to me that it was only "play like," and not to worry. It was not "play like" to me, because I could see it happening. I worried so much about that horse, I didn't see or remember much else after that.

When I settled myself back into my seat, reactivating my vice grip on the armrests, it happened again! This time Scarlet beat the poor horse to death! The darkness surrounding that scene imprinted itself on my mind and the horrible "thud" as the horse fell was a sound I was never to forget. I cried again. Back once again on Mother's lap, I pleaded, "Why is she so mean?"

After the movie was over, Mother got us Scarlett O'Hara coloring books and paper dolls. And we stopped for ice cream. The books and ice cream did not appease me, and I asked a "zillion" questions. The intense image of the poor horse in my mind did not go away...

Later that night, I lay awake wondering about the horse. I kept hearing it fall and seeing the fire, and I worried constantly about him. It would be many years before I was to understand special effects in filmmaking, but even to this day, those scenes stir the familiar worrisome memories.

As the years have gone by, I have never missed an opportunity to see GWTW and after the 122nd time to see it, I quit counting. It is my favorite movie, and I believe I could quote the script from memory if called upon to do so. Each time I see, it is like seeing it for the first time, and the two scenes involving the horse take me in memory back to a time a little girl sat gripping the armrests of a theater seat, crying over the fate of a poor old horse!

Just the words, Gone with the Wind, will always mean magic to me!

MAGNET MESSAGE:

Dear God, may we be ever aware that in all things, knowledge comes from learning, but that wisdom comes from you. In Jesus' name, Amen.

"For the Lord gives wisdom; from His mouth came knowledge and understanding." Proverbs 2:6

5. *Sweetheart and Helen*

Pick out any doll you want," the old gentleman said, as he held me up so I could reach the dolls on the top shelf of the department store's doll display.

I was three years old and I remember it vividly. I selected a beautiful "ice skater" doll with long, bouncy, blond curls, and wearing a fluffy skating costume. I was in Dallas, Texas, with Helen and her husband whom I affectionately called "Sweetheart."

Helen and Sweetheart lived across the street from us in the small town of Bardwell, Texas, where I was born. They seemed to adore children, never having had any of their own. Helen was many years younger than Sweetheart, and he seemed to me to be very, very, old. His left arm had been severed from the elbow down in a rail car accident, and I can still see in my mind the empty sleeve folded up and pinned to the shoulder of his shirt.

To me, Helen was a dear and trusted friend for as long as we lived there. She taught me to make cornbread, putting me up on the counter top so that I could watch. She let me pound on her piano, and she never got angry with me. She and Sweetheart took me on many shopping trips and let me have anything I wanted. They bought me a lovely gold sweetheart bracelet with my initials engraved on it and a dainty diamond ring in a filigree setting that I would later pass on to my own daughter.

15

But Helen's past was a mystery, as was Sweetheart's. As time went on, Mother and Daddy were to learn many things about them. Some of the things, they learned years later, long after we had moved.

Mother knew that Helen had grown up in an orphanage and had spent time in a shelter for troubled girls. Sweetheart had supposedly "rescued" her from the lonely life of an orphan, and though she was many years his junior, had taken her for his third wife. She had felt blessed and honored that he had agreed to love and care for her. But her deep yearning for a child was never to be realized. Because of this additional heartbreak, she lavished upon me all of the love she would have given a child of her own.

Just before we moved to Oklahoma City, Helen became extremely ill. I was almost five years old. I remember visiting her in her home where she lay so sick she could barely talk to me. I did not understand, and I was confused and hurt. When she died, her body lay in state in her living room before the burial service at the gravesite. Her house had a huge porch that went all the way around it, and as people gathered on the porch, I walked around watching people cry, and I saw Sweetheart sobbing. He picked me up and hugged me as he cried.

As the years went by, Sweetheart and Helen became bigger and bigger in my memory, as I made them angels in my child's mind. I cherished the gifts and the memories of them as I grew to adulthood.

Today, I never break an egg into corn meal that I don't think of Helen.I never see peppermint candies that I don't think of her because she kept dishes of them sitting on every table in her house. I often think of the walks we took and the games we

played. And I can see her face as plainly today as if she is standing beside me. There was never any doubt that "my Helen" loved me.

And then one day, my bubble burst!! When I was grown up, Mother told me more of the things she had learned of Helen and Sweetheart, and the cause of Helen's death.

The beautiful memories I had always carried from my childhood became a nightmare from which I could not awake. Helen had fallen into another life of abuse when she married Sweetheart, and it was much worse than any she ever encountered in the orphanage.

It was a sad day for me when I realized that Sweetheart, my childhood friend, the person who grins back at me in my photo album today, the one from whom I received my first kitten, the one I thought to be so kind and good, had caused Helen's death.

Helen had died of blood poisoning at the hands of her own husband when he had botched up her second abortion! It was devastating to me to learn that the Sweetheart of some of my happiest thoughts was, indeed, a double murderer!

MAGNET MESSAGE:

Forgive us, dear Father, when our actions show no respect for You and Your laws. Give us time to repent and bring healing once again to our nation. In Jesus' name, Amen.

"If men strive and hurt a pregnant woman, and she loses her child, he shall be surely punished." Exodus 21:22

6. *"Just go on home"*

I was in the first grade and miserable. I just didn't like this thing called "school," and I wanted to go home. There was safety and security in my home, and I did NOT like the "world" out there.

Kindergarten had been fun because we got to "play" all the time, and besides, it lasted only a few hours, not ALL DAY like first grade.

At recess that day, I hid in the bushes and cried. We had been in reading circle just before the bell rang for recess, and I was NOT getting it. "Spot, Dick, and Jane" could run and jump and play all they wanted to, but that didn't mean I could read about it!

I told the teacher as I sobbed, "I will NEVER learn to read!" and I asked her to be excused. She made me get back in the circle and listen. She made me hold my bookmark under each line as it was read, and I had not the foggiest notion of what I was seeing.

My mother had been a teacher before she had children, and so I knew this was not going to be easy to explain to her. It would be a big disappointment to her, but she was just going to have to accept the fact that one of her children was going to be illiterate, and was NOT returning to school!

As I stood stooped over and sobbing behind the bush that day, a grown-up sixth grade girl heard me. She came behind the

bush and put her arm around me.

"Honey, why are you crying?" she asked.

"My stomach aches," I lied.

"Then why don't you go home?"

I looked at her through my tears, and decided that was a reasonable question. So I did!

Although we lived only five blocks from the school, that walk was the longest walk of my life. As I rounded each corner, being careful not to "step on a crack," lest I "break my mother's back," I worried that breaking her back would be the least of her problems when she found out she was going to have a "dumb bunny" in the family. And, added to that was a daughter who had played hooky from school, and had even lied about a stomachache.

What was I going to do? My plan popped up easily enough in my mind, and this was it: We had moved into a new neighborhood in Oklahoma City just before I was six years old, and many houses were still under construction in the addition. One of the houses being built was right next door to us, and one of my favorite pastimes was watching the builders as they went through each stage of construction. Daddy, being a building contractor himself, had sometimes allowed me to go with him on the job and watch him build, so this was something I could do and enjoy, until school was out.

I would simply sit on the foundation of the new house until I saw the other children on our block coming home from school, and then just skip into my house as if nothing happened.

Time seemed to stop that day, and what must have been just a few minutes of sitting, seemed like hours. Finally, I decided to check on Mother. I wondered if she suspected anything. I dragged a concrete block from off the building site and pulled it into position under the living room window. It was fall of the year, the leaves were crisp, and I was afraid she heard the "crunch" under my steps as I climbed up on the block.

Mother was lying on the couch reading her Bible. As if I didn't feel bad enough already, this added insult to injury, and I silently considered running away forever! I climbed back off the block and spent awhile under our house in total blackness and silence. I finally decided to just walk in and act as usual.

Gathering up all of my nerve, I skipped up on the porch as I had always done coming home from kindergarten, and bounced through the front door.

"Hi, Mother," I called. "I'm home!"

Mother glanced up at the clock. "What are you doing home this time of day?" she asked.

I did not have the time to answer. The look on my face said it all. She always could read my mind. No sense trying to get by with anything at all. It wouldn't work. I learned that day, never, ever, to try THAT again. I got a spanking that I can feel to this day.

I would never again listen to a sixth-grader who said, "Why don't you just go home?"

MAGNET MESSAGE:

Help us recall our own childhood, dear Father, as we rear our children. They should know that we have been there, and because of that, we can help them solve their problems."In Jesus' name, Amen.

"Children, obey your parents in all things, for this is well-pleasing to God." Colossians 3:20

7. The Christmas Angel

Miss Beard was my first grade teacher. When I got to school one morning, she was sitting at her desk, her round-rimmed glasses sitting on the end of her nose. Her jet black hair was set in little corkscrew curls that lay flat against her head like a pile of tiny toy tires. She had on her usual dress of black or black print with the black shoes that seemed too large with their chunky, thick heels.

I opened the door slowly and shyly peeked in. "What are you doing here so early, Honey?" she asked sweetly, and extended her plump arms to engulf me with one of her huge bear hugs. As I made my way slowly toward her, I thought of the reason I had come so early. Mother made me do it. She said I had to go early and apologize to Miss Beard and tell her that I had told her a "big fib."

As I started toward Miss Beard, I would rather have been any place on earth except there. I dreaded to tell her what I had done, because I knew the consequences would be that I would be denied the great honor of being the Christmas Angel for the upcoming Christmas play. And I wanted that role more than I had ever wanted anything in my young life. Whoever got to be the Angel would wear a beautiful, shimmering gown, complete with sparkle wings and halo!

When I reached Miss Beard's desk, I fell into her outstretched arms and burst into tears. "Whatever is the matter, Sweetheart?" she asked as she cuddled me against her ample frame.

"Yesterday when you told us that all the girls who were finished with their arithmetic could go across the hall and try out for the part of the Christmas Angel, I went to try out. Oh, Miss Beard, I want to be an angel!"I wailed.

"Why are you crying, my dear," she asked. "You are going to be the angel."

"But I had not finished my arithmetic," I sobbed, "so I cannot do it since I told you a great big ole fib.... Mother said so."

Miss Beard took a Kleenex off her desk and wiped my eyes. She never quit hugging me as she spoke. "Molly," she said, "You will be the angel...thank you for telling me the truth."

The big night came and I felt marvelously relieved that I had told Miss Beard the truth. But the fact is, I learned a lesson I was never to forget.

Years later, Mother would tell me how hard it was to send me off early that morning to school. It was snowing, and I was wrapped up in my heavy coat, galoshes, wool gloves, and ear-muffs. She said she watched me walk down the street, head hanging low, until I was out of sight, and it was one of the hardest things she ever had to do. I had been so happy that I got the part, but I could not enjoy the excitement of it because of worrying about how I had gotten it. When I went into the house that day, Mother had known something was dreadfully wrong.

Until I was a mother myself, I didn't realize how many difficult decisions mothers have to make to teach their children valuable lessons. I am thankful for the mother I had.

MAGNET MESSAGE:

Dear Father, forgive us when we fail to live up to Your expectations and fall into the temptations around us. Help us to always speak the truth. In Jesus' name, Amen.

"...thy Word is truth." John 17:17

8. The Lost Easter Egg

Three mornings a week, when I was small, the milkman came to our back door as early as 6:30 to deliver milk, eggs, ice cream, and butter to our large family. He loaded the refrigerator with fresh bottles of Meadow Gold milk with its "goose neck" top and upon leaving, picked up the empty bottles left on the back porch.

The kitchen was always buzzing as Mother fixed breakfast, made sack lunches for all of us to take to school, and helped Daddy get off to work. The washing machine was already spinning in the corner of the kitchen, and the place was humming like a beehive.

The Saturday before Easter Sunday, the milkman always knew to bring in several dozen more eggs than usual. It took him several trips out to his truck to bring in everything when Easter was right around the corner. That was the day we colored eggs for our neighborhood egg hunt.

Mother never did spend anything on egg coloring kits for us; instead, we made our own. We put a tablespoon of vinegar-- Mother always kept vinegar on hand for rinsing our hair--in each coffee cup and then raided the cabinet for her bottles of cake coloring. We poured a different color into each cup, along with the water. Then we wrote the names of the neighborhood children on the boiled eggs with white crayons and dipped them in the colors. When the eggs were all colored and dried, we called

our friends to come over and we divided the eggs among us. All the children would have several eggs with their names on them.

I especially remember one Saturday when we had the most fun of all. We hid so many eggs that we forgot where we hid them. We made a rule that they could be hidden anywhere in our yard, or anywhere inside our house. Mother just opened the front and back doors so that we could come in and out freely as we hid them. We chose up sides and half of us hid the eggs, and the other half searched for them. We did this over and over that day, but the last "hunt" of the day ended in trouble. One egg could not be found!

Since all of us had several eggs, we put them all on the ground and counted them again, calling out the names. We finally realized that one egg marked "Steve" was lost. All 20-something kids helped search for that egg. Nowhere was it to be found. We finally decided that Lady, our bird dog, must have eaten it, and even though Steve bawled, we did finally put the incident to rest.

Months later, our family was trying to root out the cause of a foul smell in our house. I was accused of letting my cat stay in too long. Daddy was accused of sneaking his bird dog into the tub for a bath. My little brother was accused of making a stink bomb with his chemistry set, and Mother was accused of knowing what it was and not telling us.

We were all like a bunch of hunting dogs. We had our noses to the floor, the walls, the light fixtures, and into all of the closets, trying to "sniff out" the source of the stink. Not one of us thought of that ole egg...that is, until we finally were able to follow the odor to a picture hanging on the wall. There behind the picture was a smelly Easter egg marked with the name of

"Steve," and it was nestled behind the frame where it had been for many months! My little brother remembered Steve's fit when he couldn't "have his other egg," and asked us if we thought we should go give it to him!!

We finally found the source of the awful scent and removed it from its spot behind the picture. But from then on, every Easter egg hunt we had, someone would write down where all of the eggs were hidden. We never forgot that Saturday egg hunt so long ago, and we never forgot the awful smell caused by The Lost Easter Egg!!

MAGNET MESSAGE:

Dear Father, give us courage to learn from the past, work for the present, and to plan for the future...in Your service. In Jesus' name, Amen.

"I consider the days of old, I remember the years long ago..." Psalm 77:55

9. The Flavor Was Fleers

The basketball-sized bubble burst on the little girl's face, covering it and her hair! It was a mess to clean out, but the bubble made her the winner in the Biggest Blown Bubble Contest. She also got her picture in the Daily Oklahoman, although all anyone could see was that giant bubble on a pair of shoulders!

My sister and I were both Brownie Girl Scouts, and this contest was at one of our after-school troop meetings. Mother was our leader, and every Tuesday after school, we met at our home where we worked on badges, crafts, and had a lot of fun.

At that time, there was only one kind of bubble gum, and it was called Fleers Double Bubble. Others came along later, but they never duplicated the uniqueness of Fleers, either in taste or performance. About the size of a walnut, a piece of Fleers Bubble Gum was bright pink and cost one cent. The round little wad was wrapped in a brightly-colored waxed paper, twisted at each end, and on the inside of the paper was a comic.

Fleers Double Bubble was hard to find in those early years because it was said to be made of an actual rubber base, and rubber was scarce during the WW2 years. We believed this to be true because one piece could s-t-r-e-t-c-h so far. One piece had produced the basketball-sized bubble the little girl had blown that day at the Brownie meeting. Two pieces would stretch long enough to use as a jump rope! And we had actually done that, too!

My uncle, being a produce man, was able to get Fleers

when others could not. On runs through our area, he would bring us a box with one hundred pieces, and we would divide them. There were only three of us children at this time, so once divided, we made sure the pieces lasted a long, long, time. We did not know how long it might be before we got another box.

We could take pieces of the gum to school and trade them for anything we desired. Just one fourth of a piece could bring a good art gum eraser, a fat pencil, a quarter, or even a gooey cupcake at lunchtime.

The flavor was Fleers; nothing else equaled it or has since. I chewed a piece for a couple of days, then I dipped it in sugar, put the wad in one of Mother's little pimento cheese glasses, and tucked it in the refrigerator for safe keeping. I would never throw it away---not YET!

Why...a piece may be recycled over and over in the course of a few weeks, until finally, we would admit there was nothing more to salvage, and with heavy hearts, we would dispose of the faithful little "chews."

Mother always saved all of those pretty little jelly and cheese-spread glasses, and sometimes, in our refrigerator, there would be wads of Fleers Bubble Gum "ripening" in four or five of the little jars at a time--and woe to anyone who would re-move them. We each had the glasses labeled with our names and the dates we put them there.

I remember my jaws aching a lot because Fleers was strong and stiff, not soft and sugary like Bubble Gum is today. Fleers had substance! It was so tough we could blow bubbles within bubbles! When they burst, we cleaned off our faces with the wad itself, complete with all the skin oils and grime, and then popped it right back in our mouths! One piece wiped a mug many times if bubbles were popped very often.

I kept my third of the one hundred pieces in my dresser drawer. For years, the odor--and it was a delicious odor!--of

Fleers Double Bubble Gum permeated everything else I kept there. When I opened the drawer, even long after the gum was gone, I was always reminded: The flavor was undeniable FLEERS!

MAGNET MESSAGE:

Dear Father, give us patience and contentment, and a ready recollection of Your Word at all times, so that we may be an example for You. In Jesus' name, Amen.

"The Lord is good, a stronghold in the day of trouble; and He knows those that trust in Him." Nahum 1:7

10. Webber's Root Beer Stand

It was served in a tall, frosty mug, and it had three inches of foam on the top. It was supposed to be a whole new taste made of extracts from certain plant roots, and genuine root beer was said to be piped in from underground explaining why it was so icy cold.

A root beer stand, called Webber's Root Beer, stood on Pennsylvania Avenue when I was small, and it was one of our family's favorite places to go on hot summer nights, at a time when most houses had no air conditioning. Root beer was new to us, and root beer floats, served in the frosted mugs, would be most refreshing.

When Sally, my older sister, was recovering from polio and we picked her up at the hospital to bring her home so that Mother could continue her therapy, we stopped for a root beer float. I recall that my Grandmother Rogers, whom I called "Mam-Ma," was sitting on the back seat with us. "Mam-Ma," I asked excitedly. "Do you want to have some root beer?" My grandmother looked down at me and putting her arm around me, kindly and gently said, "Honey, Mam-Ma doesn't drink beer." I remember feeling embarrassed that she thought I meant real beer. After explanations, when I think back, I don't believe she really understood, because when we ordered our root beer floats, she got something else.

Years later, imitation root beer came out and was never

able to duplicate the taste of the real, genuine 100 percent root beer made from plant root extracts.

Whenever I leave the air conditioning and go out into the hot summer nights, my thoughts often go back to the time that all of us piled into the old Studebaker and drove out to Webber's Root Beer stand and Daddy said, "Set 'em up!" The carhop brought out the tray with the icy cold, sparkling, fizzing root beer mugs, and hung the tray over the half-opened window of our car.

"Oh, Boy!" Daddy said, and he'd smack his lips. "You can't beat that!" There would be no arguments against that statement from the rest of us, and to this day, even though root beer is not the same, I still think of fun family outings that often ended at Webber's Root Beer stand.

MAGNET MESSAGE:

Help us to make time for our families to be together in this fast-paced, speeding world. The time is so short. In Jesus' name, Amen.

"Take delight in the Lord, and He will give you the desires of your heart." Psalm 37:4

11. A Piece of String, Tin Cans, and a Walkie-Talkie

In the days when TV had not yet come upon the scene, neighborhoods were alive with the sounds of children running, giggling, and playing endless creative games. One of the many things I remember as a child, that we most enjoyed, was when we made a walkie-talkie.

My favorite spot was my treasured tree house, a place high in the top of a huge oak tree that grew in our front yard. The bottom branches were worn smooth from my constant hanging by my legs and the many times I scurried up its trunk.

From my vantage point at the top of this monstrous tree, I could see all around the neighborhood. When summer came and the tree burst forth with its fluffy leaves, I could hide up there and no could see me.

I built little shelves in the forks of the branches and kept all of my important possessions of the times: comics (we called them "funny books"), paper dolls, my sketchpads and pencils, and a lot of munchies. But more than anything else, I kept it for my "dreaming spot."

When I wanted to escape from the world and not be found, someone would remember my spot and then my meditation would be broken. One such person who loved to interrupt me was my little brother. He enjoyed pestering me while thinking up things for us to do. That was all right IF I was in the

mood—because, when I was, what a time we had!

"Go in and ask Mother for two tin cans," he'd say. I asked Mother, and she opened a couple of cans of green beans, peeled off the labels, and handed me a ball of string. She didn't even ask why we wanted it. She already knew.

We punched a hole in the end of each tin can, threaded the string through it, and secured it with a knot. We usually made the string long enough to "take us to Kalamazoo," Mother said.

I climbed up in the tree, Bob climbed up on the roof of the garage, and carrying our tin cans to our perches, we stretched the string as tightly as we could. I talked into the tin can I held, and Bob listened with his tin can over his ear. We could actually hear one another and pretended we were secret agents, spies, or visiting dignitaries from another planet.

The times my brother climbed up on the roof, however, came to an abrupt end when Daddy began to notice the roof leaking after a rain. "You kids been up on the garage roof again?" he asked. My brother nonchalantly mentioned that I had been pretending to be Wonder Woman and had been up there to jump off. He somehow always failed to tell that HE plastered himself up there regularly with a homemade walkie-talkie, and also when he wanted to spy on me in my tree, minding my own business.

Summer always reminds me of those happy, carefree times, when the locusts buzzed in the trees, the evenings were relaxing out under the stars, and the chirp of the crickets outside my bedroom window lulled me to sleep.

I remember, too, the times when life was not so rushed and when the price of a walkie-talkie was as cheap as a tin can and a ball of string.

MAGNET MESSAGE:

Refresh us, Dear Father, and give us opportunities to make from our memories of the past a better life in Your service for the present. In Jesus' name, Amen.

"But the meek shall inherit the earth; and shall delight themselves in the abundance of peace." Psalm 37:11

12. "Daddy, will my kitten be in Heaven?"

The little girl turned her tear-streaked face upwards toward her father's and with a desperate plea asked, "Daddy, will my kitten be in Heaven?"

The man looked down at the weak kitten, limp in his daughter's arms, and searched her tiny face as he pondered the age-old question.

He thought of the love and devotion that was mutually shared between the two of them. The kitten, a petite black and white off-the-street-stray had stolen his daughter's heart from the very beginning when she had found it--lost, cold, and abandoned in a grocery store parking lot.

The kitten was being subjected to extreme cruelty by a group of teenage boys when she pulled it from their clutches. The grateful kitten had responded with purrs and contentment and had bonded herself with the little girl immediately.

The two had become inseparable. The little cat became "Pandora," or "Pandy" for short, because, as the little girl put it, " The name means all-gift and that is just what she is to me."

Pandy had fattened up, grown a thick glossy fur coat, and her large, round lemon-yellow eyes sparkled like two golden translucent marbles. Her "motor" ran constantly, and even though the torture she had endured had left her permanently crippled, she had managed to adapt ably to her handicap.

When the little girl felt sad, Pandy was there, kneading her velvet padded paws as she licked the child's cheek with knowing condolences. They seemed to be able to read each other's minds, and they enjoyed camaraderie unlike anything her father had ever seen.

When the child walked to school every day, Pandy took up a vigil until she returned. She seemed to watch the clock, because at precisely the right moment, she would limp out to the street and head towards the school. She would meet her little mistress halfway, and even with her stiff, distorted legs, would manage to jump into her arms to be carried back home.

It was that last effort that caused injury to the little cat. In her excitement to greet her friend, who often walked too slowly, Pandy had hobbled in front of a speeding car and was flung into the air, only to fall crushed and bleeding onto the sidewalk. The vet had done all he could do. "Now," he told the child. "It is up to God."

The father stood outside her bedroom door and heard his daughter praying for the kitten. And now if the kitten died, he had the added burden of answering his daughter's heart-rending question.

"My dear," he began, as he lifted his little daughter up into his arms. "It wouldn't be Heaven, now would it, if your Pandy wasn't there?"

"I expect little Pandy here has a greater chance of being in Heaven someday than those boys who were tormenting her," he said.

The man set his relieved little girl down and noticed a look of thankfulness had spread over her tiny face. She smiled faintly as she hugged Pandy to her, and walked haltingly away, her steel leg brace glinting in the sunlight.

MAGNET MESSAGE:

If You answer the prayer of a small child on behalf of a beloved pet, dear God, how much more aware You must be of the needs of Your people who cry to You for help and healing. Give us the necessary faith to look for Your helping hand in the heartaches of our lives. In Jesus' name, Amen.

"Are not two sparrows sold for a farthing? And not one of them falls on the ground without your Father." Matthew 10:29

13. Deer Woes

I was five years old. We had just moved to Oklahoma City, and I was playing outside with our new neighbor's children. Their mother came to the door and called us to come in her house and hear a story and have some cookies.

We gathered on the sofa and the mother sat between us, two on either side of her. She opened a big picture book and began the story. To this day, I can recall only one sentence she read to us. I had to have heard the other words, though, because of the way the one sentence affected my five-year-old-mind.

The sentence was, "Get up, your Mother cannot be with you anymore." The story was Bambi, and I had fallen in love with the pictures of the liquid-eyed little guy whose image was to follow me all of my life. I could never understand how anyone could kill such a beautiful, gentle creature; let alone, EAT it!

When the lady read the only sentence I remember, I can still feel my eyes stinging as I tried not to cry. My legs barely reached the edge of the sofa, making it difficult for me to scoot off unnoticed. I quietly eased off the couch and sneaked out her back door and went home. Once in the house, and in the privacy of my room, I cried for a long, long time.

As I grew up, this was so ingrained that I became physically ill at the thought of deer hunting or eating venison. When I was in the seventh grade, my speech teacher assigned me to do a dramatic cutting from the book, The Yearling, for an entry into my first speech tournament. The story is about a fawn named Flag, so named because his little tail waves around when he is excited, like a flag in the wind.

In the story, a young boy befriends the orphaned fawn named Flag, only to be called upon to shoot the deer when Flag becomes a destructive adult.I tried desperately to do this cutting for the tournament without bawling, but I could not.

"Molly," my speech teacher said, "You must make the judges cry, not yourself."

It would be two years before I could perfect the reading enough to take it to contest and have it place in the finals.

And even many years later, the memory of Bambi and Flag etched forever in my mind, I still could not fathom anyone wanting to hunt deer or to eat them.

One Sunday, my husband and I were eating lunch with his parents, and I commented on the delicious roast.

"This is the most tender roast I have ever tasted," I told my mother-in-law. "Have some more," she urged as I finished the pieces on my plate.

"It's venison," she remarked casually without looking up. My eyes popped wide.

The permanent impressions that movies, stories, and pictures imprint on a young child's mind can never be totally calculated. So indelible was the imagery of this gentle creature etched into my brain from age five, that:

I quietly excused myself from the table that day and promptly went outside and threw up.

MAGNET MESSAGE:

May we respect all of Your handiwork, dear Father, and all of the life You have created. In Jesus' name, Amen.

"Who can ever list the glorious miracles of God? Who can ever praise Him half enough?" Psalm 106:2

14. *"We will never fuss again!"*

When my older sister stepped off the train, we grabbed each other and hugged, happily proclaiming, "We will never fuss again!" We had been separated for three long months and I had missed her something awful. My mind whirled backward to the events that had led us to the train station.

We had been visiting our cousins in a small town near Dallas, Texas, that summer when it happened. We were both learning to ride new bikes that day. Temperatures had risen to 104 degree and still we rode, long and hard, all afternoon. That night when we went to bed at our grandmother's house, Sister began to complain of headaches. In a few hours, she was running extremely high temperatures.

The next morning, she fell while trying to get out of bed, and her head was turned sideways, seemingly frozen in that position. The doctor came out from Dallas and pronounced the awful diagnosis: "It's infantile paralysis, commonly called polio," he said, "and once this crippling disease strikes, it shows no mercy to its victims, most of whom are children."

Doctors at that time believed polio to be highly contagious, so their answer to the problem was to rush Sister to Scottish Rite Hospital in Dallas and place her in immediate isolation. Sadly, I watched as they jerked off her clothes and put her in a hospital gown, chopped off her waist-length, beautiful naturally-curly hair (easier to take care of during therapy), and wheel her off from our sight.

Would I ever see her again? Would she ever walk again? We were told to go home to Oklahoma City, and they would send for us when they thought it "best." "After all, you have other children who need you at this time."

Hearts heavy, we returned to Oklahoma City. Mother stayed behind for a while, observing Sister through one-way mirrors, but Sister was not allowed to see Mother. It was thought it would traumatize her too much if torn back and forth, and if ever she were to get well, it would be best that she learn to cooperate with the treatments without emotional parents interfering. Little was known about polio, so since Sister was an experiment in cause and remedy, trusting the doctors seemed all we could do.

And now here she was, the screeching train jolting to a halt and bringing Sister back from the Dallas hospital. I knew, though, that this was only temporary and that she would not be going home with us. She was being transferred to Oklahoma City's Crippled Children's Hospital (now Children's Hospital).

Once again, she was whisked away from me and wheeled into isolation. She was measured for a leg brace and she began intense therapy immediately. We were not allowed to go to her room, but I got to wave at her from the ground outside her top-story room. The nurse pushed her bed up to the window, and I could see the tears glistening against her cheeks as she pressed her little face against the window and waved.

Finally, Mother had had enough. She marched herself right up there and brought Sister home with the promise of giving her the therapy herself. The therapy consisted of wrapping Sister's legs, neck and back in wool hot packs, since those were the affected areas. Mother dipped the wool cloths into boiling hot water, ran them through the manual wringer to squeeze them out, and then wrapped the pained and aching little 7-year-old body in them.

The wraps were so hot, Sister cried. Her skin turned red, almost to the point of blistering, from the heat. Then came the painful exercises. Just to lift her leg caused her to scream. "We will never fuss again!" took on new meaning as I hurt for her then and would have to go outside during her treatments to keep from hearing her cry.

Finally, because Mother so faithfully fulfilled the responsibility of the heart-rending therapy, Sister recovered without having to wear the leg brace, and the only outward sign that she had polio was that one leg was shorter and smaller than the other.

There were, however a lot of changes from inside the little girl. She emerged from the ordeal a miniature adult, eight years of age. Studying the Bible became her first priority and for all of her suffering, good things did come of it. She developed depth of character and faithfulness of heart, preparing her to fulfill her strong desire to be a missionary.

The depth of this inner beauty remains today, and she still is my role model, and a most admired and respected Christian lady. She continues to give her summers to teaching the Bible in the public schools in the former Soviet Union.

While as children, we did not always keep our "no more fussing" vow, we have, as grown women been always reminded as to why we hugged and said that day, so long ago, "We will never fuss again!"

MAGNET MESSAGE:

Dear Father, help us to realize that blessings can come from adversity, if we do not get discouraged and will allow You to work Your will in our lives. In Jesus' name, Amen.

"...but we rejoice in our sufferings because we know suffering produces perseverance, perseverance produces character, and character, hope...."
Romans 5:3

15. The Frosting on the Foot

When we were growing up, every Wednesday morning, our mother made one of her delicious recipes, loaded us all in the car, and we went with her to Ladies Bible Class at the church building. We went with her when we were too small to go to school, and always went with her in the summer, too.

When the Bible study concluded, the women spread out all the food they had brought, and we enjoyed our noon meal together. One thing most requested for Mother to bring was her pineapple cake with the seven-minute frosting.

On one such Wednesday morning, we were running late, and Mother put the cake between us in the front seat. I don't know why it wasn't covered. In our haste to avoid being late, I expect Mother just didn't think of it. My job was to hold the edge of the cake so that it didn't slide off the seat.

My older sister and two-year-old brother were in the back seat when my brother began to cry.

"He wants in the front seat with you, Mother," my sister said disgustedly.

"Well, he will just have to stay back there," Mother replied. "I can't drive, watch the cake, and hold him, too." And she ignored the request, started the car, and drove out the driveway.

Before we knew it, Bob had thrown that little leg of his

over the seat and stepped right smack dab into the middle of the cake with its beautiful, peaked, fluffy white icing.

Without a word, Mother turned into a parking space at the neighborhood grocery store. She opened the door, lifted the crying little man out of the icing, promptly wiped his shoe, and deposited him in the back seat where he should have stayed in the first place. But it was not without first popping his leg and reminding him to "Stay put!"

She then left us in charge and rushed into the store. She quickly emerged with a jar of marshmallow cream and plastic spoons.

Never making a sound, she opened the cream, scooped out a big blob and plopped it into the gaping hole left by Bob's shoe. Then she smoothed it over evenly all around, dropped the jar and spoon back into the sack, started the car, and we were on our way.

No one spoke a word. Mother was now in her "silent treatment mode." What would follow next, and we could predict it consistently and accurately, was her "humming" mode. The "singing of the words" mode would follow this.

It didn't take long that day for her "self-therapy" to take hold. She began with "What a Friend We Have in Jesus," followed by "God Will Take Care of You," and by the time we rounded the corner with the church building in sight, she was on the concluding one, "Count Your Many Blessings." We knew when she got to that one, we were home free. No more mad, and no more singing. We could all relax.

Through all of our growing up years, Mother's "church songs" always followed the same pattern. Depending on what we had done, the songs told their story.

If by some error of judgment, we had deeply disappointed her, the titles of the hymns she hummed and sang, all told us to what depths she was hurt.

Sometimes, it was "Be with Me Lord," "Abide with Me," or "Angry Words." At any rate, we always felt awful when those hymns started. When each one reached its peak and the grand finale of "Count Your Many Blessings," began, we knew we were safe in her acceptance once again.

I didn't eat any of the pineapple cake that day, because all I could see in my mind was the image of the frosting on that little foot as it was pulled from deep inside the cake.

MAGNET MESSAGE:

Help us, Dear God, to keep our lives free of ugliness and unkindness; helping us to have instead, the beauty of a loving, gentle spirit, so that others around us may see You living in us. In Jesus' Name, Amen.

"God is faithful Who will not allow you to be tempted above that which you can bear." I Corinthians 10:13

16. The Small Time Carnival

We called them "funny books," and our favorites were Wonder Woman, Superman, and Batman. When there were only three of us--that is, before our baby sisters were born--our most pleasant pastime was in reading and trading these funny books with the neighborhood kids. When our stack of the coveted little magazines reached over 40 inches high, Mother suggested we sell them. The plan was a great one, we thought, and it quickly evolved into the idea of a Small Time Carnival.

Daddy got out his sawhorses and cut boards to fit across them while we made "skirts" out of butcher paper to go around the edge. In huge letters, we printed the words, SMALL TIME CARNIVAL and decorated it with paper ribbon and balloons. We made up games that contestants could play, and Daddy built us little "booths" in which to display our games.

We cut out paper fish and taped a paper clip on them. We lined up poles that we made from tree limbs and attached a small magnet to the end of the string. Each "fish" had a number on it that coincided with a number on a prize. Behind the booth, one of us would sit as a player dropped his line over the edge. The magnet attracted a paper-clipped "fish," and he won the corresponding prize. We had cleaned out our toy boxes, and these toys were used for the prizes. The toys were displayed with their numbers so that children could see what they hoped to catch.

We also had a food booth. Mother got into the act by baking cookies and cup cakes, popping corn, and serving ice cold Par-T-Pak Cola. She put a muffin tin behind the food booth to keep our nickels, dimes, and quarters separated. She kept the food and drinks flowing while we took turns at each booth.

Since Mother provided the food and Daddy the props, it was understood that with this joint business venture, everyone would divide the "take." They would first have to be reimbursed for the costs they incurred, and then we three children could split whatever was left, since the marketing had been our responsibility.

The funny books were the most popular item at our carnival. Selling two for a nickel, they did not last long, and once the word spread, The Daily Oklahoman (newspaper) came over and put out a little story about "free enterprise at work in the lives of three Oklahoma City children"--and they added pictures, too.

Business went well, and before the afternoon ended, all the funny books were gone, as well as all of the food and drinks, and we had gotten rid of all our unwanted toys. We had to close up shop and turn kids away because there was nothing left. Besides, we couldn't wait to see how much we had made.

We were three excited kids when we totaled up all the coins in the muffin tins! There was $35.00!!! That was quite a huge amount back then--why, a movie ticket was just a dime, a piece of bubble gum, a penny, and a hamburger, twenty-five cents--and we really thought we were rich! (Never mind that if we had kept those original Batman comics, they are now worth thousands of dollars.)

Mother made it clear that we were to divide it equally between us. It didn't seem fair that our four-year-old brother should get as much as his eight and ten-year-old sisters, because, after all, he didn't do much except stand around grinning and looking cute and putting fish on magnets when nobody was looking. Kinda "throwing the game," so to speak.

Mother and Daddy took out five dollars for their expenses, leaving each of us ten dollars!! Boy howdy, in the lazy summer days to follow, the money came in handy for the ice cream truck, the neighborhood picture show, and of course, the Sunday church contribution that Mother made sure we took out FIRST!

Looking back, I see in that Small Time Carnival, our parents' wisdom in lessons taught us on economics, cooperation, public relations, artistic skills, and money managing.

We were learning valuable lessons in life and not even realizing it because we were having so much fun at our Small Time Carnival!

MAGNET MESSAGE:

Heavenly Father, cause us to remember daily that today we sow, tomorrow we reap. Help us to plan on it, for Your universal law of sowing and reaping is unchangeable. In Jesus' name, Amen.

"The wicked works a deceitful work; but to him that sows righteousness shall be a sure reward." Proverbs 11:18

17. *Those Amazing Shoe Machines*

I literally skipped into the shoe department of John A. Brown Store in downtown Oklahoma City when I was a child. Mother taking us shopping for shoes was such fun that even today, I can vividly recall why it was so much fun. I ran through the shoe department in order to be the first one of us on the shoe machine!

It looked much like the podium from which our preacher spoke during Sunday morning worship services, except on the backside was a little step. Behind the step was a narrow slot, through which we could slip one foot at a time. Holding on to the sides, we looked into the top of the stand and turned a knob on the side. An eerie green light would come on, and lo and behold, right there below us, we could see the skeleton of our foot! The rim of our shoe showed around the bones and we could tell how much room our feet had to grow before we needed another pair.

I used to pull off my shoes while waiting my turn to be fitted, and watch my bones wriggle and bend in the "picture" below. I was never ready to go home. It was just so much fun to watch my own bones. We made up spooky stories to go with the motions we made with our feet. To us, the machines were just a game to play while waiting for new shoes.

As the years went by, somebody along the way learned the

damaging effects of X-ray radiation, and the machines were jerked out of every store, never to be seen again. In their place came a slide rule that we stepped on, and the heel and toe slid to the size and shape of our foot. They were marked like a ruler and they measured the size shoe we required.

After the machines were gone, it was not so much fun to go shoe-shopping anymore. Gone were the days of the "ghoulish" green light, glowing in the darkness of the box with a little foot wriggling around in too-large shoes, or better yet, a little foot wriggling around without a shoe.

I just never could understand why anyone would do away with Those Amazing Shoe Machines!

MAGNET MESSAGE:

Let every success we enjoy in life be seasoned with knowledge and good judgment and reliance on You. In Jesus' Name, Amen.

"Love the Lord, all you His saints. The Lord preserves the faithful, but abundantly requites him who acts haughtily." Psalm 31:23

18. Ike

When my grandparents married, the Civil War had been over for a while, but the grief and sorrow from it still remained. As black folks, now freed from slavery, tried to find their places in a white world, many were at a loss trying to find work.

It was during this time that someone knocked on my grandmother's back door. When she opened it, there stood a black man, tall and thin, his bones protruding through taut skin. He removed his filthy, frayed felt hat with the sweat circles on the band and placed it across his chest.

"Mam, duz yo have any werk fo' a pore ole Niggah man?" His voice was hollow with weariness. His shoes were worn and filled with holes, and he grasped a tattered tapestry satchel that bulged with the contents of all he owned in the world. He was blind in one eye, and as he shuffled from foot to foot, my grandmother noticed that one of his legs was paralyzed and stiff.

"Come on in," Mama Dear--as we would later call our grandmother--told him and she called out to Papa-Dear.

Papa Dear was a farmer and rancher. Mama Dear tended a large garden and orchard, and of course, they could use help--and a lot of it!

The man's name was Ike, just Ike. No other name and no family. His parents had been slaves, and when the slaves were freed at the end of the Civil war, his relatives had scattered and

he lost contact with them.

Papa Dear built a house for Ike on land surrounding the main house. It was a one- room bungalow with a coal oil stove for cooking and a potbelly heater that burned wood for heat and cooking. A screen door kept out the insects and let in the breeze during the summer. Ike was hired to help chop weeds, pick cotton, butcher meat, take cattle to market, and cook meals. And by the time my mother was born, he had also been Nanny to eight children, with two more to come.

My mother was only three years old when Ike would carry her up the twenty-two stairs to her bed, only to have her giggle and run back down to have him do it again.

"You devilish chillun," Ike would say, "are jest drivin' me crazy!" And he chuckled under his breath.

When Mother and her nine siblings grew up and married, all of us grandchildren loved to repeat the game and pretend we were asleep so Ike would have to carry us all the way up the stairs, too. Ike would stretch his mouth wide in a toothless grin.

While visiting there, we loved to go out to his house and sink down into the big feather mattress Mama Dear made for him. Then he would pull up a chair and tell us Bible stories by the light of his lantern.

Ike loved to sing and hum. He taught us Negro spirituals, songs passed down from slavery days when singing to God was a way slaves ended a dreary day.

In the evening, we often heard Ike as he made his way down the cobblestones to his house. Swish--plop, mmmmmmm, swish--plop, mmmmmmmm he hummed, keeping time to the sway as he dragged his leg.

Papa Dear paid Ike once a month and that day was a red-letter day for all the grandchildren who lived in the small town and those who came to visit. There were twenty-four of us

when we all got together, and Ike brought back candy and gum for us, just as he had done for Mother and her brothers and sisters when they were little.

When I married, Ike was beginning on the third generation of "his chillun," and the cycle was starting again.

By the time our second child was born, he had fallen into ill health. He left his front door open during the summer that last time I ever saw him and when I walked down the sidewalk in front of his house, I heard him humming. I peeked inside to show him my new baby and to see how he was doing. It wasn't long after that visit that Ike left us. Although no one knew for sure, most folks thought Ike was well over 100 years old! The state of Texas bought most of Papa Dear's land when they plowed a four-lane highway through it. Along with the once-rich cotton soil, Ike's house and the land on which it sat were leveled.

Today, when I drive down that highway, it is hard to keep my eyes on the road. I am searching for the spot where the little house had been, where the lantern had glowed through the screen door, and where the humming of "What a Friend We Have in Jesus" could be heard as it floated out into the evening air.

MAGNET MESSAGE:

Guide our lives that we may make one life better for our having been here. May our influence be one that is in line with Your will in all things. In Jesus' name, Amen.

"A faithful man shall abound with blessings." Proverbs 28:20

19. Miss Feather

Two eyes, pupils dilated with terror, glowed from behind the bushes. The frightened little animal hissed, pinning back its ears and crouching low against the ground as I parted the bushes to get a better look.

I was in the third grade at Creston Hills Elementary School in Oklahoma City, and it was recess. I had noticed a group of sixth grade boys poking something in the bushes with sticks. I could hear from its cries before I ever got there, that it was a kitten.

I have loved animals all of my life, but cats just happen to be my favorite pet, so when I heard one in trouble, I ruffled up my 8-year-old nerve and chased off the 11-year-old boys.

Behind the bushes, I saw a filthy, crying, half-grown kitten whose color was questionable because of mud matted together with burrs in her coat. Some of the burrs had burrowed down to her skin, causing her great pain. She was so terrified that as I reached out to her, she spread her claws and lashed out at me. As the bell rang, I softly told her that if she were still there when school was out, I would take her home.

Back in the classroom, I could think of nothing else. I fidgeted in my seat for the next two hours. "Please, God," I prayed, "let her still be there when school is out."

Finally, the bell rang and I ran to the cloakroom, grabbed

my book satchel and lunch pail, and headed straight back to the bushes on the playground.

"Hey, little kitten," I called, and I pushed aside the branches. There she was, all twisted up in the long thorny limbs, crying pitifully.I crawled in behind the bush and began the task of freeing her--it was difficult--the thorns pressing deeper into her trembling body. Finally, I managed to get her out. Taking her home on my bicycle proved to be next to impossible, so I pushed my bike home instead of riding it.

The next few days I spent combing out burrs, treating bleeding skin, and brushing the little orphaned kitten. She was soon purring and relaxing as I handled her.

It was about this time that a girl named Judy Ann moved into our neighborhood. She had a weird voice, and the other kids made fun of the way she talked and the muffled sounds that came from her throat. Because I didn't make fun of her, we became close friends. I allowed her to help me care for Miss Feather--so named because after the "clean-up," I found myself with a gorgeous, gleaming white, feathery soft kitten with sky-blue eyes. Judy Ann loved Miss Feather as much as I did, and she seemed to understand the little cat that soon grew into an elegant feline with a sweet and humble disposition.

One day, Mother suggested that I give Miss Feather to Judy Ann. "You have other cats; Judy Ann doesn't have any. She lives close enough that you can still visit her. Don't you want to share?"

I thought about the suggestion for a long while, and then reluctantly agreed to do it.

As most of us "cat people" know, a pure white cat with blue eyes is almost always deaf. Miss Feather was no exception.

I had learned early on that the little cat could not hear me. She needed constant care and attention because of this handicap, and Judy Ann seemed to be the one who could help watch and protect her.

Judy Ann was overwhelmed when I told her that she could have Miss Feather. She hugged her, and the cat purred happily. Judy Ann was well aware of the extra care Miss Feather would need, and she wanted to give it to her.

I knew in my heart that I chosen wisely Miss Feather's destiny because Judy Ann, like Miss Feather, was also stone deaf!

MAGNET MESSAGE:

Dear God, in all things, whether they be great or small, we see the loving hand of Your providence. In Jesus' name, Amen.

"He raises up the needy out of affliction." Psalm 107:41

20. Uncle Arnold's Grocery Store

When I was a little girl, my favorite place in the whole world was my uncle's grocery store. It sat square in the middle of Main Street in a little town in Texas that boasted of a population of "600 wonderful people, and one old grouch."

Wooden breadboxes lined the sidewalk in front of the store, and old-timers sat on top of them, leaning back against the wall, while chewing and spitting. I watched where I stepped along the tobacco-spattered walks when I opened the creaking screen door to go inside. A bell hanging from a string tied to the top of the door jingled faintly as it announced my arrival

There were twenty-four cousins when we all got together, and Uncle Arnold gave us "grazing rights" to the store. He allowed us to go back to the butcher shop, cut a slab of baloney and cheese and make ourselves a first class Dagwood sandwich with fresh bread right off the shelf. We could build it as high as we pleased with the fresh produce out of the bin, and he let us snack on candy bars, chips, and all kinds of snacks.

My cousins all lived in the small town, and we were the only "outsiders"; therefore, the store held a fascination to me that the others took for granted. I thought it was just the grandest thing in the world to pull an ice-cold Coke out of the big red-

and-white steel chest, because Cokes were "special treats" allowed only on special occasions at home. The chest was filled to the brim with chunked ice, and to reach 'way down into it would leave my hand numb. The opener was attached to the side of the chest, and I popped off the cap, turned up the sparkling green bottle and gulped down its cold contents.

Uncle Arnold let me pick any candy bar I wanted, but I usually chose a moon pie and a package of peanuts to put pour into my coke.

Since it was usually summertime when we visited there, a giant fan, high in the loft above the store kept the air moving enough to give some relief from the hot summer days.

Uncle Arnold had to stack things to hold them down so they didn't blow around the store. There was a section in the back where the racks displayed comics. We called them "funny books," and if I could keep the pages from blowing, I could read them while I drank my coke with the peanuts in it.

It was in the back of the store that a ladder led up to the loft. We climbed it, carrying our sandwiches, snacks, and soda pop up to relax in front of the fan while we ate.

In the winter, old-timers, instead of sitting on the breadboxes outside, gathered around the open flame stove, sipping hot coffee, and spinning their tall tales while playing games of Forty-Two.

Today, the tiny town has become a suburb of Dallas, Texas. A new Main Street has been built, and modern grocery stores have sprung up all over the town. When I visit there today, I have to search for the old Main Street, and try to figure out just where Uncle Arnold's Grocery had been.

As I walk down the remains of the brick street with grass

growing between the bricks, my eyes are busily scanning the boarded up buildings that are barely still standing.

Suddenly, I see a familiar sight! The rotten old boards, nailed across a leaning building fail to conceal the faint lettering, dimly outlined above what used to be a door.

Although the building is covered with graffiti, as I walk closer, my heart racing, I can see the weatherworn words, "Arnold's Grocery," barely legible as though trying to escape from another dimension. It is then that my mind goes back to a time when those words were synonymous with love and home, and the memories engulf me with their warmth and sweetness.

MAGNET MESSAGE:

Give us humility of spirit and kindness of heart as we go from day to day trying to serve You. In Jesus' name, Amen.

"...be thankful and bless His name." Psalm 100:4

21. The Hat with the Streamer

The sermon seemed exceptionally lengthy that Sunday morning, and having to sit still and quietly for so long a time was difficult when I was eight years old.

I was dressed in my finest Sunday clothes, and Mother had topped off my outfit with a darling little hat that had a long satin ribbon streamer in the back.

While I sat against the back of the pew, the ribbon was so long that it would catch behind me, jerking the hat lopsided. So when we sat down just before the sermon was to begin, I tossed it over the back of the seat where it hung down into the hymnal rack behind me. Then I settled myself for the long-winded sermon.

I wonder why Preacher's Kids--P.K.'s we always called them--seem to be the most mischievous, because that is where I made my mistake with the hat streamer! Our P.K. was behind me!

I tried to look pious and dignified, but I was aware of the activity going on behind me, because Bill Banister kept crawling under my pew and pulling my shoelaces. I was not allowed to budge during the worship, so I sat rigidly enduring his goofy capers until someone made him get back up on his seat. But he did not stay here. Next on his agenda, and what I did not know, was that he was not only tying knots in my hat streamer, but he also was stuffing the end of it into the hymnbook.

The requirement to sit very still in church services, coupled with the length of the sermon, caused my head to tilt back slightly and my eyes to close, causing me to be the perfect, immobile candidate on whom Bill Banister could perform his aggravating antics.

When the sermon finally came to an end and we all stood to sing, my hat jerked off my head, flew backwards over the seat, and onto the floor, dangling by its streamer, still lodged in between the pages of a songbook.

Bill Banister laughed so hard--out loud--that he was escorted from the auditorium. I was too embarrassed to turn around, and I just stared straight ahead, trying to appear as if nothing had happened. Mother turned around, retrieved my hat, and plunked it back on my head, knots in the ribbon and ALL!

Every Sunday, it was so bad, I would request that we sit somewhere else if Bill Banister was anywhere in sight. I think he purposely waited to see where we would sit before he came in so he could slide into the spot directly behind me. I never knew what he would do next. Sometimes it was my hair hanging over the seat that brought out all of his mischief. He loved to tie it up too, and hold it down when I got up. He untied my dress sashes when the congregation stood to sing, he tossed spitballs over the seat into my lap, and untied my hair bows. I think his mother must have been worn out and pretended not to see, or else, in her exhaustion, had just fallen asleep.

The hat with the streamer also had a feather at the band where the ribbon attached, and Bill Banister loved to pull it out and tickle my cheek. He would lean up and put it under my nose to make me sneeze, and leaning back, would thump me on the head.

I often wondered whatever happened to Bill Banister and if he ever spent time in juvenile delinquency court. I've heard that he is a reputable attorney somewhere in Texas, but I wonder if his children pulled stunts during church when they were small, comparable to the stunts their father pulled as a child. I'm confident that they, too, probably loved to pester a little girl with long hair, a hat streamer, sashes and ribbons while she sat in church trying to act indignant--but underneath it all, loving every minute of it!

MAGNET MESSAGE:

Dear Father in Heaven, help us to realize that if we seek Your approval daily, we will never have to worry about Your disapproval. In Jesus'name. Amen.

"...for whatsoever a man soweth, that shall he also reap." Galatians 6:7

22. Lightning Bug Fever

Lightning bugs! For several years, I have not seen the tiny critters, and had almost forgotten about them. Lately, however, they seem to have made a comeback. About dusk every evening, I see the little lantern lights everywhere, just as I used to when I was a child. It brings happy memories as I sit in the backyard watching my cats chase the ever-darting insects that continually evade their grasp by shutting off the light just in the nick of time.

I remember how difficult it was for me to catch them when their shine vanished. In my child's mind, I thought the bug itself had just disappeared, giving me the feeling that somehow the small insects were magical.

When I was small, all of us grandchildren would gather on our grandparents' lawn when our grandmother opened up her ice cream freezer. She made the most delicious ice cream flavors from her fresh fruit and her hand-milked cow's milk, and nothing tasted better on a hot summer night. Especially after all that "lightning bug fever," when we chased the little rascals for hours on end.

We got our grandmother's canning jars from her canning house, and pursued the evasive little glowing mobiles until we were exhausted. When we got the jar full, we would lie down on the grass and watch them glow. By the time darkness fell, we played like we had a homemade lantern as we watched the contents of the jar blink on and off like a flashing neon light.

We also learned that the light rubbed off and continued to glow afterwards. We rubbed it on our fingers and made glowing "rings."

As I sit in the backyard and think on these things, I wondered if the bugs have been here all the time and I am just seeing them again for the first time. I just haven't seen so many in a long, long time. It took me back to the day when I was a child and suffered from "Lightning Bug Fever." It was a pleasant memory.

MAGNET MESSAGE:

The simple things in our lives often bring the sweetest thoughts. Thank You for these. In Jesus' name, Amen.

"Thine is the day, Thine also the night; Thou hast established the luminaries and the sun." Psalm 74:16

23. On Being Always Thankful

As children, we were taught to be thankful in all things, but a child, unless he has something with which to compare his life, cannot always comprehend the meaning of "thankful."

Mother instructed us at an early age on the definition of "thankfulness," but I never came to appreciate the full meeting of it until I was nine years old and in the fourth grade.

When the need arose in the Oklahoma City school system for a teacher to finish out a moving teacher's term, Mother was called. She had quit teaching when her children were born, and she had not intended to return. The Oklahoma City Board of Education had, however, pleaded with her, stating the desperation they felt in trying to find someone to teach in a very difficult area.

The area where there was a need was the poorest section of the city. Several families with babies and children of all ages lived together in one-room, drafty, leaking shacks. Illiteracy and truancy were rampant, and the physical needs of the children were as urgent as were their educational needs.

Mother decided to accept the challenge, but at the same time, she considered her own children. She was able to arrange to transfer us to another school so that the four of us could ride to and from school together, so that never at any time would we be at home without her.

That year proved to be a learning experience that none of us would ever forget. When we visited Mother's school, the children considered my sister and me "princesses", and they all wanted to touch our ribbons and dresses. As they stared at us in awe, they would sigh about how "lucky" we were.

Mother always made our dresses and while they were not fancy, she always frosted them with hand-made tatting, embroidery, rickrack, or lace, and to those little girls, we were nothing short of royalty.

I remember especially wintertime and the cold, skinny, bare legs I saw protruding out from under thin dresses with ripped and hanging sashes, and no winter coat to cover them. I recall feeling very embarrassed to wear my heavy, wool coat.

Mother did all she could to help the little ones in her class, and they adored her. I watched her many mornings carry dresses and bags of toys to the car. And once when she stopped by the house of a boy who had been absent, she found him hobbling around barefooted with a bloody rag around his foot. She learned he had been digging for worms to go fishing, and his brother had accidentally chopped off his big toe. Gangrene had set in, and if Mother had not checked on him, he might have died.

This same little boy's mother was home that day trying to feed her baby powdered milk from a baby bottle. She could not read the instructions on how to mix the powder with water and the baby was starving. I watched as a grateful mother cried when Mother showed her how to mix the formula with water to feed her baby.

Mother encouraged us to use our earned money to buy Cheerios® at lunch so that we could save the wrappers. Returned to the company, according to instructions, the wrappers were the same as money. A Cherio was ice cream on a stick dipped in chocolate, and rolled in nuts. I ate so many that year, I grew sick of them. BUT I turned in 600 wrappers, and that did not include the ones my siblings saved and the ones we gathered out of the trash cans everywhere we went. There were enough to get some really nice gifts for her class, including one bicycle. In return, the children brought Mother "gifts" of candy bars they had saved for her. The candy was wormy, and the children giving them had no idea it was not perfect. They thought all candy was like that.

I was relieved when I finally didn't have to see the devastation, utter and complete hopelessness, and the sad little faces again. I tried to pretend that since I could no longer see them, they did not exist. But the reality never left me, and I am sure Mother taught us, by allowing us to see other lives with which to compare ours, not only compassion and sharing, but the true meaning of being always thankful.

MAGNET MESSAGE:

May we be always thankful, Dear God, not just on Thanksgiving Day, but every day of our lives. May we always be ready to help those less fortunate than we are. In Jesus' name, Amen.

"Enter into His gates with thanksgiving and into His courts with praise; be thankful unto Him..." Psalm 100:4

24. *Raising Quail*

It is early morning during the spring and summer that I hear the quail whistling their bobwhite call in the tall grass fields behind our house. Their catchy little trill instantly brings to my memory two little quail that Daddy bought to set himself up in the "quail raising" business when I was a child.

"Now you kids are NOT to make pets out of these two," Daddy warned. His plans were to raise a covey of the delicate little birds to turn lose on eighty acres of land he had purchased down by Noble, Oklahoma. His hopes were for the birds to "be fruitful and multiply," thereby guaranteeing him abundant game for hunting on his own land when quail season rolled around every year.

When we named the pair, Quincy and Quaila," Daddy realized that his warning was going to go unheeded, and that he might just as well have saved his breath.

We loved to sit down by the pen and watch the birds, and they became so tame and used to us that they hopped up on the top of their shelter, stretched their necks and whistled "Bob White" to their heart's content. We sat close enough to touch them through the chicken wire, and we whistled right back to them. When Quaila laid thirty-five eggs, we were ecstatic! Quail eggs are about five-eights of an inch long, and the tiny birds that emerge are perfect replicas of their parents. Unfortunately,

Quaila's eggs had a hard time hatching that first year. The shells were too thick and tough and the little guys couldn't get out.

We crawled into the pen to help her and, of course, by then they were tame enough to allow our assistance. Daddy took his pocketknife and very carefully, made slits in the eggs so that the chicks could peck their way through. Even with our help, only seventeen managed to survive. The others had simply been in too long and had either died in incubation, or died of exhaustion from trying to emerge before we could help them.

Daddy was already beginning to see his predicament. How, he wondered, could he turn lose pet quail on land and then hunt them? What possible sport could be involved in going up to a tame quail and shooting it? And eating it? It was an impossible idea. He began to realize that raising quail was not such a good idea, especially when you have young children.

When it rained, Quaila puffed up like a balloon, made her "calling" noise and all seventeen of her soft, round children got under her. I will never forget the adorable sight of that small mother bird with seventeen tiny faces peeking out from her fluffy feathers. I thought of the Scripture that says,

"How often would I have gathered thy children together, even as a hen gathers her chickens under wings, and you would not." (Matthew 23:37)

We watched the little ones grow up, learn to whistle their familiar notes, and soon, they too, were answering our whistles as their parents had done.

We had watched Daddy labor long hours building the pen in back of the garage and securing it for their safety before he ever brought Quincy and Quaila home. We knew that he had spent quite a lot of money in building it, and we knew he was disappointed to have to do what he had to do. Gone were his dreams of a hunting paradise on private land on which only he could hunt.

With all of us looking on, Daddy loaded up the bird family and together, we drove out to a protected area and turned them loose. We had to stomp the ground to get them to move away from us.

I remember worrying about the birds late at night, but Daddy always assured me that they would be all right if they never did fly away to other areas. I like to think that they lived out their natural life span in protected grass, never having to run from hunters' guns and dogs.

I never hear the call of the bobwhite that I don't think of Quincy and Quaila--and Daddy raising quail!

 MAGNET MESSAGE:

As we look around us let always be aware of Your hand-prints on everything we see in Your mighty creation. In Jesus' name, Amen.

"I commune with my heart in the night; I mediate and search my spirit." Psalm 77:6

25. Old Lady Stewart

When we were growing up, the boys in our neighborhood always called her "Old Lady Stewart." We girls thought that was disrespectful, but we didn't try to stop them. In our hearts, we agreed. Mostly WE called her "Old Maid Stewart," which was a term used for a woman who never married. It's no wonder she never married, we giggled; there wasn't anyone who would have her.

We thought she must surely have a pointed black hat, crooked teeth, and a wart on her nose .No one could ever get a good look at her, and we didn't want to.

We saw only the swift movements of the curtains, or heard a door slam shut when we walked by, but mostly we saw her dog! He was a GIANT German Shepherd, and he protected her yard like a 300-pound security guard would protect Fort Knox. But we had a big dilemma: the lot on the other side of Old Lady Stewart's was vacant, and it was a perfect place to fly our kites or mark off our baseball diamond. BUT we had to pass the old lady's house to get there.

We spent a lot of time devising plans to get over there without attracting HER or her DOG. It wasn't easy. We finally figured out we could go around the block the other way and come up on the vacant lot from the back. This was difficult, too, though, because that dog was always watching, and Old

Lady Stewart was, too. IF we made it to the vacant lot, we had a wonderful time. We flew our kites, sent "messages" up the string, pretending to contact aliens, and spent many hours scraping off weeds to make a ball diamond and to mark the bases.

But always, always, we would see Old Lady Stewart's curtain flutter and see her shadowy figure at the window. She gave us an eerie feeling.

One hot summer evening, we heard the screeching of brakes on the street right in front of her house. Neighbors came out to see what had happened. Lying bleeding in the street was the old lady's dog, "General," who had been hit by a speeding car!

Shocked, we held our breath as the old lady came out of her house. She was not a witch, and she did not have crooked teeth and a black pointed hat and warts on her nose. She was a woman grieving over the loss of her beloved pet. Suddenly we felt very ashamed as we watched her try to move the dog off the street. Tears streaming from her eyes, she had some of the neighborhood men help her bury General in her back yard. As we walked away, a tremendous feeling of guilt swept over us. How lonely Miss Stewart must have been, and how much more lonely she would be now.

We banded together, made cookies and favors, and took them to her. It wasn't nearly so frightening to go up on her lawn now, and when she opened the door, her eyes lit up with joy. She was a petite woman, and her voice was kind and sweet. How in the world had we built such a wild story around her?

That was the beginning of many visits with Miss Stewart that all of the children in our neighborhood came to enjoy on a regular basis.

One day builders came to finish out the addition, and they built a house on the vacant lot that had been our ballpark, and one day Miss Stewart didn't come to her door when we went to see her. She was found later that day. She had died in her sleep, clutching the little stuffed doll we had made her, and a genuine sense of sadness filled our hearts.

Sometimes things are not as they seem to children, and on that day so long ago, we learned a valuable lesson from "Old Lady Stewart."

MAGNET MESSAGE:

Give us compassionate hearts--ones free from making judgments in situations we don't understand. Allow us time to live out that compassion and understanding in our lives before it is too late. In Jesus' name, Amen.

"Discretion shall preserve thee, understanding shall keep thee." Proverbs 2:11

26. Saundra's Duck

A ll of our young lives, Daddy often came in from work and asked us, "Well, Kids, how's your conduct?"

As we began to give him a rundown of our conduct for the day, he always finished by saying, "Well, it had better be above reproach." We knew exactly what he meant when he asked that and we knew exactly what we had better say.

However, he often asked other children the same question when they visited us, and they had not the foggiest notion what he was talking about. He would chuckle as he listened to them try to figure it out. It embarrassed me so much that I always tried to change the subject.

There was a little girl named Saundra who lived across the street, and she had received a baby duck for an Easter surprise one year. Back then, we could go to the TG&Y and buy baby chicks, ducks, and bunnies that had been dyed pastel colors for Easter.

When the ducks and chicks outgrew their city homes, parents often took them to the zoo and turned them loose to live. Saundra's duck was cotton candy pink, and she adored the soft, downy little creature.

Every day you could see Saundra skipping along, "Doofus" waddling right behind her.

One crisp fall morning, Daddy went out on the front porch

to get the paper. He heard a noise coming from the direction of Saundra's house. Looking over there, he saw her on the steps, head buried in her hands, tears spilling down her plump, rosy cheeks.

"Hello, there Saundra," Daddy called. "How's your conduct?"

"Oh, Mr. Rogers," sobbed Saundra, "Mother took my duck to the zoo!"

MAGNET MESSAGE:

Thank you, Dear Father, for the innocence of little children. Their sweetness and gentle spirit can teach us so much. In Jesus' name, Amen.

"Suffer the little children to come unto Me...for of such is the Kingdom of Heaven". Mark 10:14

27. The Beauty of the Lord's Day

Church bells rang out loudly all over Oklahoma City when we were children, and Mother would say, "It's because it is the Lord's Day." In the summertime, our windows would be open (no air conditioner then), and the sound drifted into our house, loud and clear, beautiful and reverent. The bells put us in a quiet and peaceful mood as we got up and dressed for Sunday School and church.

The sound of the bells calling people to worship came from St. Luke's Methodist Church. The church, known for its magnificent belfry, caused surrounding churches to respond with ringing chimes. All of them together made Sunday morning a concert or chorus of clear, concise bells and chimes. What a pleasant way to begin a new week as the sound could be heard for miles around, pealing out its message against the beautiful blue sky with its clear, clean air. The entire city seemed to bask in the afterglow of the harmony long after the ringing had ceased.

Saturday was always a day of preparation for the Lord's Day. We were allowed no "fun" activities until all of us had studied our Bible lessons and answered the worksheets. We had to be sure the laundry was done and the lawn mowed. There would be no click-click of the hand-pushed lawn mower or any fluttering of clothes on the line on the Lord's Day. Mother always made sure the cabinets were full of groceries, and Daddy made sure the car was full of gas by Saturday evening. Since there would be absolutely nothing open on Sunday, if we planned on eating or driving anywhere, we made sure we had arranged for it ahead of time.

On Sunday afternoon, after all of the worshipers had returned, our neighborhood fell silent except for the trill of the locusts in the trees in the summer, or the whistle of wind around the house in the winter. A peaceful aura over the entire city with its deserted streets settled calmly and quietly as most everyone honored the ONE, to Whom the day belonged. The day was an oasis in the desert; restful, relaxing--a refresher course in what life is all about and why we are here.

It was a day to give us steam to face a new week and strengthen our armor against the undesirable forces of darkness. It was truly a day of respect, devotion, allegiance and -- reverence. It was a day that seemed to bring neighbors closer.

Sunday was also "pot roast day." All our neighbors seemed to leave at the same time, and opening their doors, it was as though all of us "synchronized" our pot roasts, because the aroma was one huge smell that sent us on our way not only rejoicing, but our mouths watering, as well.

All of these things: bells, chimes, respect, the reverent atmosphere, deserted streets, closed businesses, closeness of families, the worship assembly, and that ever-present aroma of pot roast, bring to my memory, The Beauty of The Lord's Day--as it used to be. . .

MAGNET MESSAGE:

May we once again love, honor, and respect You and Your Day as the One to Whom love, honor and respect are long overdue. In Jesus' name, Amen.

"I was in the spirit on the Lord's Day..." Revelation 22:9b

28. The Leaping Leopard

Lincoln Park Zoo in Oklahoma City held a magical fascination to me as a child growing up near there. Our family visited it often, and I could easily slip into another dimension of time watching those magnificent animals. I thought I could read their minds, and it was nothing for me to spend more than an hour at one cage. I would study their every move, the look in their eyes, and I would even pretend that I could crawl in there with them and pet them.

My favorite pens were the ones that housed the great cats. I especially loved the leopards. I admired their sleek beauty, their graceful movements, and their incredible muscular structure. As I stood up on the rails, I leaned as far over the rail as I could without hanging upside down. As I hung there and talked to them, I was completely oblivious to anyone else being around me.I was brought back to consciousness when Mother came to get me. If we got lost from each other, the rest of the family always knew where to find me.

Then one warm summer day, the police cars came driving slowly down our street. The loud speakers were on high volume and the police kept repeating:

"Please get your children off the street and into the house; a leopard has leaped out of his cage at the zoo and is in this area!" The police were armed with threatening-looking guns,

and the lights spun around as the sirens screamed between announcements.

Sheer panic broke out in our neighborhood. Children scurried about like ants on a hill, and screeching and running in all directions, they rushed into their houses, slamming doors behind them. Curtains parted, venetian blinds opened, and the children sat in front of their windows for a ringside seat. All of the children ran--except me. I was not about to go in the house and miss a chance to pet this beautiful creature. I couldn't understand what all the ruckus was about. So I parked myself on top of the brick planter surrounding our front porch, and ignoring the police warning, waited for the opportunity of a lifetime! If I saw him, I would simply call him, and he would come to me and purr...I just knew it.

I felt not one shred of fear as I sat and waited. As I think back on that scene, I know that the kids who went in their houses and sat with their noses pressed to the window glass were mostly curious to see if I was going to be eaten. I just thought they were silly.

I will never forget what happened next. The leopard came strolling down the middle of our street! How gorgeous he is, I thought. Just as I was going to jump down off the brick wall to run and pet him, sharpshooters felled him with one shot to the head!

"NO!" I screamed and jumped off the planter and ran to the street. The police had everyone get back out of the way, as neighbors came easing out of their houses, one by one, to watch the elegant feline die. The officers picked up the bleeding cat, and throwing him into the back of a truck, sped off. The remaining crew cleaned up the mess and took down the barriers

they had placed around the street. I don't remember ever feeling such rage as I felt at that moment.

A taxidermist in Oklahoma City stuffed the beautiful leopard, and for a time he stood on a pedestal in the east wing of the Capitol building. I used to walk over there to see him. I stood and looked into the cold glass eyes, studied the features of strength and stamina, and tears filled my eyes. In what would be his final bid for freedom, the leopard had jumped twenty-five feet up and over the log railing that had imprisoned him for over ten years. I reached over the guardrail and touched the once-lustrous coat, and ran my fingers over the velvety nose.

At long last, I was petting the leopard...

MAGNET MESSAGE:

In Your scheme of things, dear Father, there is a purpose for all of nature. Help us to realize this and to respect Your creation by never wasting these marvelous resources. In Jesus' name, Amen.

"Rejoice in the Lord always. Again I say, rejoice." Philippians 4:4

29. Snow Ice Cream with Cherries

When we were children, we often wished upon a star. The little verse was: "Star light, star bright, the first star I see tonight; I wish I may, I wish I might, have the wish I wish tonight."

After we had said the little rhyme, we could not look back at the star, or the wish might not come true. My older sister and I would often lean on the window sill of our bedroom window after the house was all quiet for the night, and gazing skyward, wish upon the first star we saw. We then quickly lowered and closed the Venetian blinds so that we wouldn't be tempted to look back at the single star which would grant our wish.

I remember in the wintertime, wishing it would snow. I loved to walk in the snow, play in the snow, sled in the snow, ride a trashcan lid down a snowy embankment, build a fort in the snow, make snowballs, and build snowmen. But most of all, I loved to EAT the snow. Our mother could make the best snow ice cream in the whole world. I remember sitting at school and daydreaming out the window as I watched it snow, excited about the surprise Mother would have for us when we all got home. It was so nice to come home and have her there every day. The atmosphere was warm and cozy, and there was always something that smelled good coming from the kitchen when she greeted us at the door.

On snowy days, however, we could predict the awaited

surprise. There would be a tarp spread outside, covering the freshly-fallen snow to protect it from the paw prints of all my little feline friends, and the huge dishpan, hanging on its nail on the back porch, would be waiting for us to fill it with snow.

As we bounded in the door on snowy days, we literally skidded across the freshly waxed hardwood floors, bringing in the snow with us. We often caused a delay in our ice cream treat by first having to mop up the melting snow.

We grabbed the old dishpan and ran into the back yard and scooped up as much snow as possible without getting any dirt in it, and hauled it back into the house before it began to melt. Mother would have the eggs, sugar, vanilla, and milk mixed and ready to receive the glittering, fluffy stuff. She whirled it around with her wire whisk, beating it to a smooth, creamy consistency, and served it to us topped with chocolate syrup, nuts, and cherries if we wanted it that way. Sometimes we preferred it plain, but I always wanted more cherries on mine than anything else, and I don't recall anyone ever worrying about the fact that the eggs hadn't been cooked.

Snow ice cream with cherries was my favorite dessert. Even now, when I watch a gentle snow falling in the winter, my mind goes back to the times when I was a little girl, and a simple wish on an early evening star sometimes came true.

MAGNET MESSAGE:

For the glittering beauty of Your creation: the snow, the mountains, the streams, the sky, stars, and the sunshine--for it all, we are truly thankful and blessed. In Jesus' name, Amen.

"Have you entered the storehouses of the snow...?" Job 38:22

30. The Bite of Revenge

Loyalty ran high in our family growing up. We could say all of the nasty things we wanted to say about our siblings if we got mad enough, but no one else had better say anything bad about any one of them!

I loved my little brother dearly and would have run through a three-ring fire for him, but we loved to tease and aggravate one another. He is four years my junior, and when we had a fight, it was a humdinger; but when we "made up," we were best friends.

During one period of my childhood, I had imaginary animal friends who could talk. I made up stories about them and Bob wanted to "see" them, too. I pretended that only I could see them, and he would become furious when I told him that. Of course, watching his rage only encouraged me to mock and tease him that much more, and I told him that only certain people could see them "and you, Bob, are not one of them."

Once during an outbreak, he grabbed my arm and bit me! Mother was across the street visiting a neighbor, and I screamed, "I'm telling on you!"

But Mother kept staying across the street. I waited and waited. The bite mark began to vanish. I waited some more, and soon the mark was completely gone. What would I have as proof that her "pride and joy" had, indeed, bitten me?

I had a glorious thought! I went into my closet, shut the door, and placing my teeth directly over the spot, proceeded to bite my arm as hard as I could! I had to replace the mark so Mother would believe me. She stayed so long that I recall having to re-bite it several more times before she came home.

When she finally came through the door, I ran to show her my arm with the teeth marks on it. Bob got a spanking! You would think I would have been happy with my "bite of revenge," but I was not.

I felt so sorry for him. Revenge was NOT sweet and I also felt terribly guilty. All of our childhood, if I received a spanking, Bob would cry, "Please Mother, don't spank her, spank ME instead." I thought about that and I felt awful.

As a result of that encounter, I had to confess to Bob that I really did NOT have a mouse friend who lived inside the shower wall, and that I had just made up all of those stories, loving every minute of his fit-throwing. I thought he was so funny when he got mad, and laughing at him made him even funnier. No wonder he bit me!

It was awhile before I told Mother the whole truth of the matter. My conscience had eaten me up about it, so I finally got up the nerve to tell her. To this day, I cannot remember her reaction, but I expect I got to pick a switch--as I always did--from off the back-yard peach tree.

 MAGNET MESSAGE:

Father, forgive us when we disappoint You and help us to overcome the daily temptations with which we are often confronted. In Jesus' name, Amen.

"The wise man's path leads upward to life..." Proverbs 15:4

31. State Fair Daze

Git chur Oklahoma State Fair Tickeeets!" the wiry little man with the squeaky voice screamed as he strolled up and down the sidewalk on Main Street in downtown Oklahoma City when I was small. It was an exciting time in a child's life back then when the Oklahoma State Fair came to town for its annual run.

The fair grounds were located at that time over on North Eastern where Douglas High School is now. We lived just about two miles from it, and we would gather up all the neighborhood kids and hike out there. Mother packed us a lunch, and we got up early, so we could get there when the gates opened.

I had $5 that I had earned just for the fair tucked safely in my pocket. I had helped around the neighborhood--feeding pets when owners were gone, or helping clean out a room when someone needed help. That $5 would take me on all the rides; give me plenty of cotton candy, caramel apples, etc. Plus, I might even get a souvenir--like a cap with my name embroidered on it.

When we ten or so kids entered the gate, we split up in twos, but because we were all interested in the same area, we were still "running into each other." The place we always headed first was the "magical midway!" The row of flapping tarp murals that covered the entrances to the sideshows enticed us with their paintings, advertising shows featuring The Snake Lady, The Man with Two Heads, and the Donkey Lady. As we

sauntered on down the midway, our mouths gaped open with awe at the "Freak Shows," as they called them.

For a dime, we could go in and stare at people who made their living this way. We expected to see someone who was literally half-snake, only to see a poor soul who had a severe skin rash, giving her a scaly-like appearance. The imagination had to be stretched really far when we saw unfortunate people who were born deformed and felt they could survive no other way. I recall a sad feeling sweeping over me every time I went into one the shows, but it did not keep me from going back year after year. I always thought, "One of these times, I will REALLY see a half-snake person."

I especially remember the furor one midway act caused. Billed "Sally Rand and Her Fan Dance," it was rumored that this dancer removed all her clothes and hid behind a feathered fan at the end! We stood outside and listened to the barker try to lure all of us to go in. For a sneak preview, Miss Rand would come out onstage dressed in a feathered bikini with her huge fan, and the barker would say, "To see more, come on in!" The boys in our group rushed eagerly up to the ticket taker, dimes in hand! The rest of us were dying of curiosity. Did she REALLY undress? We were never to know, because the boys kept it a dark secret. I expect it wasn't as "exotic" as they had hoped, or they would have boasted about it. Instead, they just kept us wondering by giggling and whispering all the way home.

I especially remember one year at the fair when I wanted to take home a present for Mother. All I had to do was toss a dime into this beautiful crystal (cheap glass, actually) dish, and it would be mine. How easy, I thought, so I trustingly handed the man my ticket. I tossed a dime into the bowl, only to have it slide down the side, spin around, and hop right out! It came so close, I must try it again, I thought. I did... again...again...and again! Soon my entire $5 was gone, and I had not even been on the rides or the midway shows. I was one unhappy little girl, and I just wandered around the rest of the day, sad and miserable.

When we got home that evening, I tearfully told Mother that I had ALMOST won her a "beautiful crystal fruit bowl." Then I told her about my $5. "That was gambling," she told me. I really didn't understand, but I knew that was a "bad word," and I knew I had the same as "thrown away" my hard earned $5! It was a valuable lesson, learned early in life that has stayed with me. Especially was it a good lesson when I later learned that the game is "rigged" so that no one ever wins. From then on, every year at the fair, I stayed away from the "games," and concentrated on my favorites, The Fun House and the rides!

When the state fairgrounds moved to their present location, it ushered in a new era. The Midway, as we had known it, was gone, but by then my tastes had changed, and it didn't matter anyway. My interests then lay in the exhibits and crafts; the loud noises and excitement the Midway held for me as a child were no longer a part of my State Fair Daze!

MAGNET MESSAGE:

Dear Father in Heaven, if we do not learn from our mistakes, we are destined to repeat them. Give us every opportunity to learn from them the first time. In Jesus' name, Amen.

"Create in me a pure heart, O God, and renew a steadfast spirit within me." Psalm 51:10

32. Cartwheels and High-heeled Shoes

Mother, why don't you come turn cartwheels with me?" I asked her one day when some friends and I were turning cartwheels down the middle of the street in a race to the end of the block. I was about ten years old, and Mother always said that she wouldn't know how to act if she looked out the window and didn't see my feet sticking up in the air! I flipped and flopped my way through my preteen years, forever standing on my hands, doing the splits, and turning cartwheels. It was a happy, carefree time in my life as a child.

"I'm just too old and stiff, I guess," Mother said in answer to my question. "Humph," I muttered to myself in disgust, "I will never be too old, nor will I ever get too stiff," and I walked off in disgust.

"Mother," I would ask again. "Why don't you ever wear high heeled shoes like Miss Nicholson"--Miss Nicholson was a grade school teacher, and she was young and beautiful---"instead of those old thick clunky heels you wear?"

"I would probably fall and break my neck if I wore those skinny heels," was always Mother's answer when I asked her about her thick-heeled "old-lady oxfords," as I called them. I wanted a mother who was modern, glamorous, and fashionable, one who painted her long nails red, wore platform heels like Betty Grable, had hair down to her waist, kept it dyed, and who could turn cartwheels.

"Humph," I would grumble again. "When I am grown, I will wear high heels and I will wear them no matter how old I am."

The years flew by as years do, and as adults, we are often called upon to eat the words we once spouted loudly and clearly as youths. It pays to just never say what you will or will not do, because you will probably do precisely the opposite. I suppose a wise woman just keeps her mouth shut.

Wise, I was not. Determined, I was. The cartwheels ceased when I turned fifty and had, with aching joints, continued to turn them just to prove a point and keep a promise to myself. No one needed to know that the cartwheels almost broke my back and pretty near wrecked my wrists.

The high heels are different. That is one promise to myself that I continue to keep. Never mind the cracking ankles.

Years later when the podiatrist told my mother that she had the "best feet I've ever seen," because she had always worn "sensible shoes," I looked at my worn and weary feet and wondered if it had been worth it. Because "sensible shoes" always seemed to be thick, heavy, and ugly, I convinced myself that yes, it had been worth it.

Recently, a young niece of mine asked, "Aunt Molly, why don't you ever turn cartwheels anymore? You taught me to do them, and now you don't do them anymore." "Well...I guess I got too old." I decided to be honest.

"Humph," I heard her whisper under her breath as she walked away. "I will never get too old!"

And the cycle began again. . .

MAGNET MESSAGE:

Forgive us when vanity gets in the way of common sense. Help us to keep our eyes on the cross and our hearts in tune with Yours. In Jesus' name, Amen.

"For thou dost require a man according to his work." Psalm 62:12

33. *Sunday Morning Wake-Up Call*

F resh and hot, right out of the pot,
    The best you ever got!
    They shine your teeth,
    They curl your hair,
    They make you feel like a millionaire!"

"Now...who wants the first one?"

These are the immortal words of our daddy, who all of our lives, was the self-appointed chef on Sunday mornings! Pancakes were his specialty, and he would call us to breakfast with the above rhyme, which he had used as a child calling people to his corner hamburger stand.

We all had to wait our turn for the next batch because a large family in a one-bathroom house had to rotate shifts of eating, showering, and getting ready for church services. We would all get up at the "wake-up call" except Mother, and nobody knew when she had gotten up, or if, in fact, she had ever even gone to bed. (Not one of us remembers Mother ever being in bed.)

When we got up, we found our shoes polished, our dresses pressed and laid out, along with matching ribbons, sox, and clean underwear. Our brother's suit and our daddy's suit were fresh from the cleaners, and the dining room table was already set for Sunday dinner. There were extra places set in case someone may want to come home with us. The roast was in the oven, vegetables on the stove, salads and deserts in the refrigerator, and rolls rising on the counter tops. Somewhere in between all that, Mother got dressed and ready for church by the time we children got the "wake-up call"!

We would order from Daddy the number of pancakes we wanted, eat them at the breakfast nook, clear the table, do the dishes, shower and dress, and by some miracle, all be ready to leave the house just in time for Sunday School. The last one of us out the door had to make sure the door was UNlocked in case a neighbor got home before we did and needed to borrow something.

Today the old pancake grill is still stored in its place of honor. It is totally black, and there will never be an attempt to scrub off all of those memories. The very sight of it brings to my mind the vision of my dear daddy standing at the stove, flipping pancakes and whistling. I can still hear the whistling as it stops, and a booming voice awaking me from my pleasant dreams:

"Fresh and hot, right out of the pot,

the best you ever got!

They shine your teeth,

They curl your hair,

They make you feel like a millionaire!"

Now...who wants the first one?

MAGNET MESSAGE:

Grateful thanks, Dear God, for the gift of a mother and father who set good examples for us. In Jesus' name, Amen.

"A good man obtaineth favor of the Lord." Proverbs 12:2

"A virtuous woman is a crown to her husband." Proverbs 12:4

34. *"You left a shell in the gun!"*

O ne, two, three, four..." I counted as I lay on my bed late at night when I was a child and Daddy had come home from quail hunting. I could not go to sleep until I heard his truck pull into the driveway, heard him come through the back door, and heard the shotgun shells hit the hardwood floor as he unloaded his gun!

I kept very still and counted them as they hit, and if there was a pause, or I did not count as many as I thought there should be, I would scream out in panic, "Daddy! You left a shell in the gun!" Then he would shove the bolt, and no sound of a shell hitting the floor would allow me to hear for myself that there were no more shells in the chamber. Although I was always glad to see Daddy so happy when he got to go quail hunting and bring home his "limit," I always dreaded quail season because I worried so much about him. I was afraid he might fall and his gun would go off, or that he would think he had emptied his gun and one killer shell would remain. I could not rest until he was safely home and the gun unloaded! Only when I was positive the gun was empty could I relax, turn over, and go to sleep. That is why I always counted the shells as they hit the floor.

Daddy had always been an avid quail hunter; so much so that while other families enjoyed the traditional turkey at

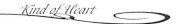

Thanksgiving, our family always had quail. Flanked by huge platters of the golden fried birds, Daddy would exclaim, "Oh, boy, the Lord sure knew what He was doing when He fed quail to the Israelites!" We never failed to get the Bible lesson as Daddy bit into the delicious, delicate, little white-meated birds.

Daddy loved to fish too. "I have a lot of good talks with the Lord when I fish," he always said. "I feel closer to Him out there on the lake than anywhere else!" Indeed, his very life before us children exemplified that he had talked with the Lord...and OFTEN! His life was one of example and truth. His word was his bond, and the reputation he enjoyed as building contractor verified that. He was often sought as a builder because of his honesty and integrity. "He's the only person I have ever known to whom I would just turn over my checkbook," a man whose house Daddy was building once said. In fact, he later did just that!

Daddy could have been rich if he had built houses like others did. I remember how worried he would be when he saw other builders order low-grade lumber and charge superior-grade prices, and how it bothered him when other builders rolled up the steel reinforcement in concrete driveways AFTER FHA inspected them, and then pour the concrete without it. "The customer doesn't know the difference, and my houses look just as beautiful outside as yours do," they would tell Daddy. "You'll never get rich building the way you do," they added.

We watched, as children do, all of this as we grew up, and it did not take us long to realize what a priceless father we had. Because his standards of integrity were so high, it was often hard for him to find help to measure up to his expectations. Therefore, most of the time, after he figured a job, did the blueprinting, and got the house started, he ended up doing most all of the carpentry work, too. "There's only one way to be sure it gets done right," he'd say, "and that is to do it yourself."

Daddy was an excellent Bible student. We always felt we could ask him anything about the Holy Scriptures. When we did ask a question, though, we had better be prepared for a long sermon, because we always got more than we had asked. He always knew both chapter and verse for all our inquiries. "Remember now your Creator while you are young..." (Ecc. 12:1) somehow always ended being quoted, regardless of the question we had asked. It was his favorite scripture.

It was difficult to disobey a father like ours. He expected so much that we tried to always rise to the occasion. For me, that was not always possible, and I remember how brokenhearted I would be when I knew I had failed him. He never raised his voice and he never screamed at me. The hurt look out of those expressive mahogany-brown eyes was all it took to reinforce the guilt I already felt. To make me realize I had hurt him was the best preventive measure he could take against my ever repeating the offense.

It has often been said that the greatest gift a man can give his children is to love their mother. We all had no doubt about how much Daddy loved Mother, and we never questioned his love for us, either.

A mother's influence as the heart of a home has long been realized, but only in the last few years has a father's influence as the soul of home been appreciated. How blessed and thankful we are to have had a home built on the solid foundation of equal portions of both heart and soul!

When blindness ended forever Daddy's happy hunting

days, and his last and favorite bird dog died at age 14, as much as I had always worried about him during hunting season, I honestly began to wish I could once again listen for his truck. That I could listen for his footsteps, and the bolt-action slide on his gun as the shells hit the floor and I counted them. I now know that many times, he purposely paused while emptying his gun, just to see if his Number Two daughter was still awake and listening, for he knew she would scream: "Daddy! You left a shell in the gun!"

Thank you, Daddy, for the wonderful Christian example you always were to us, and for giving us the treasured gift of your unblemished name! I pray that none of us ever causes you grief by dishonoring it. Happy Father's Day!

This column was my Happy Father's Day tribute to Daddy in June 1995.

35. The Quilt Box

Daddy was contracting and building houses when we were small, and we thought he was an artist! His trim work and cabinets were as much a work of art as was the finest painter's creation on canvas. With all the swirls and twirls and curly-cues he added to his cabinets, I thought when he painted them white, they looked like mounds of Mother's marvelous divinity candy.

Therefore, it was only natural that for a wedding present, he had made Mother something out of wood. So, 64 years ago, he built her a beautiful cedar-lined quilt box, which I recall always standing in the living room, where it served not only as a storage for quilts, but a deacon's bench as well.

One day, all of us neighborhood kids decided to play "Kick the Can," and it began to rain. We kept playing because we loved playing in the rain as long as it was not an "electrical storm." We could build dams at the end of the street, causing the waters to collect until the puddles were deep enough for splashing and wading.

But this rainy day, Mother was next door visiting her friend, Mrs. Mason, while Mrs. Mason's son, Steve, played the game with us. When all of us had been "caught" except Steve, we kept waiting for him to "set us free" by kicking the can, but he never did come. We began to get worried.

We called and called...to no avail. Finally, Mother came home and called us in. She said we were wet enough and that Steve was probably playing a joke on us. When we went into the house, the quilt box lid popped open, and out jumped Steve! He was so proud of his hiding place that he was grinning from ear to ear!

Steve was not only sopping wet, and his feet covered with mud, but everything in the quilt box was too. He had wormed himself all the way to the bottom of the chest, leaving his soggy, muddy trail on all of Mother's quilts and our winter clothes.

I have never in my life seen Mother as mad as she was then! She didn't even sing her "church songs," like "Count Your Blessings," the way she always did when she felt she needed to be reminded of how many she had. I guess at that moment she couldn't think of any, because she came mighty close to whopping someone else's child!

During the springtime, Mothers always took our wool skirts and sweaters to the cleaners, and then she carefully stored them in the quilt box with mothballs to keep them fresh until time to wear them again in the fall.

I will never forget the look on Steve's face when Mother finished with her "tongue lashing." Then he had to go home for another one. He was quiet for several days, and we didn't see hide nor hair of him. But Steve Mason was one hardy fellow. He came back in full force not too long afterward, and we never knew what he would do next. He was the neighborhood comic relief, but many times the humor was not realized until years later.

MAGNET MESSAGE:

Help us, Father, to be less self-centered and more God-centered as we live day to day on this earth.In Jesus' name, Amen.

"He that is slow to anger is better than the mighty..." Proverbs 16:32

Kind of Heart

36. Texas League Park and the Oklahoma City Indians

The old ballpark stood surrounded by a wooden slatted fence full of knotholes and rotting wood. But I loved that old park. It was where Daddy took us on summer evenings to watch the Oklahoma City Indians play when we were children. It was called Texas League Park, and we always sat in the bleachers where it didn't cost too much for our whole family to go.

My favorite ball player was a man named Al Rosen. Old Al approached the plate, put the bat between his knees, reached down and dusted his hand with a white powder--I never did know what that was--and gripped the bat tightly. He then made a giant sweep into the air, and bringing down the bat, made an X on the ground in front of him where he wanted the ball to go. He made more home runs than anybody else, and he was my hero.

My next favorite player was Ray Murray. Ray lived in our neighborhood, and he made a game of putting baseballs into his pockets to give to us for souvenirs. I still have one that the entire team signed. I stood outside the locker room one evening after a game and waited for the team to come out and autograph my baseball. I took it home and covered it with clear nail polish so that the names would never fade.

I remember sitting in those bleachers and being fascinated by the overhead garage door advertisement that hung above the park fence on the opposite side. All through the game, the door would open and close as it advertised the ease with which you could operate an Overhead Garage Door. The entire fence was covered with advertisements, but that garage door pitch is the one I remember the most.

We loved to sit in the bleachers. More than once, I scrambled out onto the edge of the grass to try to retrieve a foul ball. If one landed in the bleachers, a lot of kids had to fight me to get it.

We pestered Daddy for hot dogs, cokes, and popcorn. I know now the cost was not the only reason he took us to the bleachers. We wriggled and ran around so much was probably the real reason. It was a big picnic to us because we knew many people there. Even though there was a lot running around going on, I never failed to whip to attention when Al Rosen got up to bat!

Bill Fountain was the newscaster for WKY radio back then, and we always got to see him there, too. As he left in his WKY car, he waved at me one night, and I thought he was just so handsome.

On the nights we didn't go to the games, Daddy made a score sheet and kept score at the breakfast room table. He placed the radio in the window so we could listen to it while playing outside. Mother popped corn and mixed up lemonade, and we piled on a blanket to do cartwheels when Al Rosen made a "homer"!

Today when I go over to see Daddy and he is sitting close to the radio, listening to the 89'ers play, and talking to the team-

--just as he did so many years ago to the Oklahoma City Indi-ans---I am suddenly a little girl again, sitting in the bleachers of Texas League Park, and it is a fun memory.

MAGNET MESSAGE:

Today is the day of joy for us, Dear Father, as we know not what tomorrow holds. May we put our all into living each day as a gift from You. In Jesus' name, Amen.

"Boast not thyself of tomorrow, for thou knowest not what a day may bring forth." Proverbs 27:1

37. The Day a Fight Began

My brother, Bob, was just about the cutest little guy you would ever see. He was the only one of five that Mother called her "pride and joy." And you would think with a title like that and the only boy in the group, he would be spoiled. He was not.

But, there was just something about his nature that brought out the orneriness in us. Maybe it was his habit of crying and talking at the same time, or maybe it was just his being the minority in the group, and therefore, an easy prey.

Anyway, when he was six and I was ten, I remember an incident that I will never forget. Mother was going to have to run to the store, and she very carefully laid out the rules she expected us to follow while she was gone. This did not mean, by any stretch, that we would abide by them, but we certainly did intend to try.

She had not been gone ten minutes until Bob and I had an argument. I do not remember what it was about, but I chased him out the front door and locked it behind him. Then I quickly ran to the back door and locked it, too.

We had the strangest doorbell. It made a piercing ring that was so shrill that we often covered our ears when someone pressed the button. That day, to aggravate me even more, Bob put his thumb on the button and just held it down. I thought the noise would drive me nuts, so I pulled the breaker-switch on the back porch, cutting off the electricity. He kept running around the house trying to get in, bawling and talking to himself as he ran, and since I found this profoundly funny, I laughed at him.

Not long after turning off the electricity, I noticed water running out from under the refrigerator. The ice was melting in the freezer compartment. When I began to mop up the floor, I heard a loud crash. Bob was banging on the glass door at the back porch. As I peeked around the kitchen door, I saw the glass shatter into thousands of pieces! Left around the edges were splinters of sharp, jagged glass, still in the frame of the window.

"Oh...what are we going to do, Mol' Lou?" Bob asked me as he peered through the shattered window. Just as suddenly as the fight had started, we joined forces to become instant friends again. It was no time to continue to fight. It was time to call a truce. So we did.

Now the problem was how to get out of this mess. Bob went to the garage where Daddy kept his tools and got his hammer. We knocked out all of the splintered pieces and swept up the mess, kicked on the electricity, and mopped up the wet floor....all just in the nick of time.

Mother drove into the drive, and we carefully closed the screen door over the glass-less window, hoping she would not notice.

She brought in the groceries and placed them on the table. So far, so good. Bob and I exchanged glances and tried to distract her by bringing in the rest of the sacks. This, of course, was unusual behavior, so she immediately suspected something was going on, but just like Bre'r Bear did, Bob and I "lay low."

Mother began to sing church hymns as she always did when she was upset and her nerves needed quieting. But she said nothing. By the time Daddy got home, all was quiet on the home front, and Bob and I thought we were home free.

Not so. The minute Daddy walked into the house, he bellowed, "What in the world happened to the glass in the back door?" (We sneaked outside, quietly and undetected.)

"Oh," Mother said, "Molly Lou and Bob got in a fight while I was at the store and broke it out." Very calm. No yelling. No mad spell. Just those eternal "church songs." And that constant humming...always humming. Why didn't she just spank us and get it over with?

"Well, they get to pay for it out of what they earn," Daddy said. It would be days before we were allowed to tell what had happened. They waited until all had settled down, and then when they asked us what went on that day, we both began to talk at once, each blaming the other one for the broken window! The fight was on again...

MAGNET MESSAGE:

Dear Father, keep us from wasting time by being an excuse-maker, and keep us from blaming others for our mistakes. Rather let us work hard to accomplish Your will for our existence. In Jesus' name, Amen.

"Create in me a pure heart and renew a steadfast spirit within me." Psalm 51:10

38. That Boy

"Who dumped the trash on the front porch?" Mother asked.

"It was That Boy," we replied.

"Who keeps ringing the doorbell and running off before we can answer it?" Mother wanted to know.

"It's That Boy!" we answered.

Indeed, all of the mischief in our neighborhood when we were small could be credited to That Boy.

That Boy lived on the street behind us with siblings ranging in ages 6 months to 14 years, and they all seemed to be everywhere at the same time. But That Boy was the same age as I was, and we were in the same class at school.

I remember one year especially well when I was in the fourth grade. Even though all the children in our neighborhood usually walked to and from school together, I did all I could to avoid him. He had no personal hygiene habits, and I often wondered if he even owned a toothbrush. This particular year, That Boy somehow got a "crush" on me. I spent recesses hiding from him. Those clouds of odor surrounding his presence made all of us want to hide. Since I did not want to be unkind to him, he had gotten the false notion that I returned his feelings. Because of this, he spent many hours creating schemes he thought would catch my attention.

The morning I remember so well, it was pouring rain all

day. Back then, we had a "cloak room" at the back of the schoolroom, and each of us had a hook for our coats, gloves, umbrellas, etc. That morning I hung up my raincoat and umbrella and sat down on the floor to remove my galoshes when That Boy came in.

"I'm gonna KISS you today, Molly!" he said with a proud and boastful arrogance as he bent down to speak into my ear.

I didn't say anything, but sheer terror shot through my being, as sharp as if a bullet had struck me! If he succeeded in kissing me, the yellow stuff on his teeth would surely come off on me and I would die. And what would Mother think?

Thankfully, the rain continued all day so that recess was called off. Now all I had to do was face the walk home. I began to plan my defense. I would simply hang behind and walk home the long way.

When school finally let out that day, it was still raining. I bundled up in my raincoat, got on my boots, picked up my umbrella, and hid. After a reasonable amount of time had passed, I slipped out the back door of the building. Just as I rounded the corner, That Boy jumped out and grabbed me!

"Ah-ha," he squealed! "You thought I'd gone, didn't ya?"

I jerked away and ran as fast as I could go! I let down my umbrella as I ran, and when he gained footage, I hit him with it! I then ran up on a porch and banged on the door! No one came. It was too late. That Boy yanked me by the hair, jerked my head back, and kissed me square on the mouth! I could feel the yellow sticky stuff on his teeth against my lips.

"Told cha I'd kiss ya!" and he laughed gleefully as he ran on ahead.

One million germs had invaded my mouth! I was going to die---I just knew it! I walked the rest of the way home, thoughtfully reflecting on whether or not my life was in order. It had

better be, I thought, because I am fixing to leave it!

I did not move my lips. I held my mouth in the same position, afraid to lick my lips or to swallow, because I knew I would fall down, right there on the street in the rain, and expire-- no one would ever know what had happened.

When I finally got home, I walked through the door, my mouth permanently frozen in its germ-laden position, and between clenched teeth, I told Mother:

"Help me. That Boy kissed me!" Without a word, Mother got the soap and water. She washed out my still-opened mouth, working up such lather that I could literally blow bubbles! I must have rinsed a hundred times before the bubbles finally ceased.

After I brushed my teeth several times, I was pleasantly surprised to see that I was still very much alive and had not been murdered by the sloppy smooch after all!

I don't recall That Boy ever bothering me again.I guess I scared him to death with my hysteria, and later the family moved from our neighborhood.

The entire area of Oklahoma City called "Creston Hills" seemed quiet after That Boy moved away.

MAGNET MESSAGE:

Just for today, Dear God, let me be kind to someone who needs it most and try to understand when someone needs a friend. In Jesus' name, Amen.

"Above all else, guard your heart, for it is the wellspring of life." Proverbs 4:23

39. Dinner with Abbott and Costello

The roaring applause almost popped off the roof of Oklahoma City's Municipal Auditorium that night in 1946! It was exciting to me, because the applause was for my older sister, Sally.

As I watched her timidly make her way toward the front of the massive stage, I thought back to how she happened to be honored there that night!

"Sister," as I have always called her, was a polio survivor. It had changed her life in so many ways; one being that she was forced to give up physical activities that she was no longer able to do. To compensate for this loss, she filled the gap by becoming an avid reader and writer. She spent many hours with her Bible, books, and magazines. It was in one of her magazines that she learned of a contest sponsored by Lou Costello. Lou was the half-wit half of the Abbott and Costello comedy team that was at the peak of their popularity at the time. The contest was an essay contest with the topic being, "How I Would Fight Juvenile Delinquency in America."

Lou Costello lost a two-year-old son in a drowning accident, and the contest was in his memory. Sister entered the contest and wrote an eloquent essay, sprinkling it with Scripture, and other bits of wisdom gleaned from one who had suffered a disappointing setback in her life. She wowed the judges with her

spiritual insight and maturity. She was eleven years old!

Sister was one of ten winners in the state of Oklahoma. The prizes consisted of a private dinner with the two comedians, a medal with their pictures engraved on it, cash, and on-stage recognition from the two men.

Now the shy pre-teen was finally on the stage with Abbott and Costello beside her. After their comedy routine performance, they received the ten winners as their guests for dinner.

Following this exciting evening, Sister began to write for Playmate Magazine, a, pre-teen magazine of the times. One of the articles she wrote was the story about getting to meet and dine with Abbott and Costello. Lou Costello's daughter, Paddy, wrote to her inviting her to take a cruise with them on their private yacht. They remained for many years, pen pals, and good friends.

The thundering applause still rings in my ears as I think of that joyous night for the self-conscious little 11-year-old who "just happened to enter a contest."

 MAGNET MESSAGE:

Let us always look to You, God, for guidance in our lives, and to always give You the glory for whatever blessings come our way. In Jesus' name, Amen.

"Trust in the Lord with all your heart, and lean not to your own understanding." Proverbs 3:5

40. *"Good Morning, Mrs. Howell"*

The blackboard in Mrs. Howell's fifth grade classroom was filled with the daily work she expected her students to finish. At the very top, written in big, bold letters, was the Bible verse for the day. Beneath it stood the American flag, erect and proud on its stand, and as the bell rang, the children filed quietly into the room.

"Good morning, Mrs. Howell," the children said in unison as one by one they went to their desks and stood respectfully beside them.

"Good morning, children," Mrs. Howell said in returning their greeting. She then led them in their morning prayer, read them the Bible verse, and they repeated it after her. Then they said the Pledge of Allegiance, and all were seated at the same time.

"It's time to take up books," Mrs. Howell told the children. The new girl visiting the class was Mrs. Howell's niece whose school had already recessed for the summer. It was fun for the girl to go to school and have her aunt be her teacher. It was just as much fun for the girl to visit Mrs. Howell's home. It was a paradise of books, and after a week there, she still would not have seen all the treasures in Mrs. Howell's bookcases. Everything in her house was a learning experience for the girl. The American and Texas flags, high atop tall metal poles, flew proudly in Mrs. Howell's front yard. Her love of God, family, country, and TEXAS was never questioned. Taped on her dresser mirror, the girl always found a little card with scripture printed on it. It was changed daily, as was the scripture on the blackboard at school.

At school, Mrs. Howell not only taught reading, writing, and arithmetic, but she taught children right from wrong, honesty, kindness, the rewards of hard work, responsibility, and loyalty. She never set standards for her students by which she herself did not live.

The children all loved Mrs. Howell, and they showered her with gifts. For over 50 years, Mrs. Howell taught school, and was often called out of retirement. She kept every pair of earrings, every bracelet, card, and trinket the children gave her, and she could remember who gave each one to her.

Mrs. Howell was an avid reader, kept up with current events and could discuss any subject, with anybody, anytime. She continued this practice beyond her retirement until a stroke erased most of her short-term memory. She once commented on what she saw as the unjust and disgraceful way the Negro race was treated during those years. In all kinds of weather, the little black children would run behind the school bus, not allowed to ride with "whites."

"Now you KNOW that just can't be right," Mrs. Howell would say.

Today, at 93, Mrs. Howell resides in a senior village, her legs rendered useless by the stroke and her mind capable of remembering only that somewhere, sometime, she had been a teacher and character-builder of children. Every day from her wheel chair, she still "teaches," and if you should pass her room, you probably will hear her say, "Good morning, children."

MAGNET MESSAGE:

Thank you, Father, for loving teachers who set impeccable examples and expect no less from their students. In Jesus' name, Amen.

"...Be thou an example..." I Timothy 4:12

41. Twenty-One Cats!

It was raining that day as I sat in the attic sifting through the memories in the boxes that were stored up there. I had chosen a rainy day to do this because, sitting close to the roof, the soft pitter-pat of the rain caused a peaceful, quiet, calmness to settle over me, making the keepsakes found there even more alive and sweet.

One of the boxes contained a little book with a pink, padded taffeta cover. As I slowly opened the book, I read, written in Mother's beautiful penmanship, my name, under which was a lovely poem called "Baby Mine."

"Baby Mine, oh, too soon you'll roam, Baby Mine, far away from home," it began. "The things that Mother did for you, will then in turn, be yours to do," the poem continued.

Inside the pages, Mother had written down "cute" things I said as a child. It was detailed, like a story, and a photo was glued beside each episode. As I read the things that Mother, as a young woman, had written, my eyes filled with tears. I felt as though I was a visitor into the private thoughts of my mother as I read each installment of love.

As I stared at the book, I was taken back in memory to the childhood about which my mother had written, in this, my baby book. In every picture of me, no matter my age, there were cats or kittens in the picture with me.

There was one of me pouring milk from my baby bottle for a kitten. There was one of me sitting on a blanket in the yard with kittens spilling all over my lap. There was one of me at age two in my Easter frills, and the picture is blurred. A kitten walked by just as the camera shutter went off, and I had bent down to pet it, blurring the picture.

As the book's pictures took me back, I remembered when I got old enough to have my very own kitten, of how I got her, of how much I loved her, and how I promised myself that as long as I lived, I would never be without a cat. I thought of the many times I had brought home injured cats. Mother expected it every day. Most of the time, though, it was a homeless little waif who "just followed me home" (with a little help from me!).

The black-and-white kitten that came to be my constant companion for twelve years had so many kittens during those years that I lost count of them. When it came time to give them away, I would beg and plead to keep them because I could not bear the thought of someone else having them. A litter would grow up and have kittens and the scenario would be repeated. When the total number of my cats grew to 21, the neighbors complained, the birds disappeared, and Daddy said, "Something has to be done!"

With sadness and regret, he asked me to pick out two kittens to keep along with my original mamma cat called "Maw-Cat." The decision had been impossible for me to make, and I cried all day and night until the decision had to be made for me. Daddy locked me in the bathroom while he rounded up eighteen cats and kittens for the trip to the Humane Society! It would be a long time before I realized how hard that was for Daddy to do.

Sitting there in the attic, I recalled my saddened spirit and heart that day. As the rain began to pound harder on the roof, I was reminded of all the tears I have cried over my cats, but also reminded of all the joys they have given me. I reflected on old "Maw" and how I sneaked her into the window at night to sleep with me; of how she always came to meet me as I walked home from school, and if she had kittens, they followed her to meet me, walking single file behind her.

A huge clap of thunder jolted me back to reality and the baby book, which I was still holding. As the blurred words came slowly into focus, I read, "Baby's first word." On the line, Mother had written, "Kitty."

MAGNET MESSAGE:

Dear Father, for whatever purpose You gave us pets, I am thankful. They bring such simple joy and happiness.In Jesus' name, Amen.

"A righteous man cares for the needs of his animals, but the kindest acts of the wicked are cruel." Proverbs 12:10

42. Roy, Trigger and Me

y Hero. My Knight in Shining Armor. That was Roy
Rogers to me. I was eleven years old and in love with
this singing cowboy--a cowboy who could settle any
scuffle, a cowboy who was the symbol of all that was right and
decent in the world.

Every Saturday afternoon at the neighborhood theater, for
ten cents, my heart would race with excitement, as my Hero, on
Trigger, would dash across the screen in magnificent splendor!
It was amazing how Roy would not bounce an ounce in that
saddle, Trigger never did get hit by flying bullets, and the forces
of Good always won! I would feel all warm and safe inside as I
daydreamed myself right into Roy's and Trigger's lives.

I covered my bedroom wall with Roy's pictures, at a time
when others were covering their walls with a new idol called
Elvis. When Roy married Dale Evans, I felt rejected and jealous,
but I added his wedding pictures to my wall collection, and I
clipped every picture I could find from newspapers and magazines to hang there.

Then I heard the marvelous news that he was coming
through Oklahoma City to make a quick personal appearance
while on his honeymoon!

Like an arctic blast, I hit the front row of the Tower Theater in Oklahoma City on that cold winter night toward the end

of the 1940's. I sat fidgeting through two movies waiting for the all-important appearance. Finally, after his show, when he came on stage very briefly, I made a dash for the stage door that opened out into the alley. I pushed aside a policeman who stood blocking the door; he lost his balance and fell! I couldn't stop to apologize--I HAD to make it out to the alley before Roy got in that cab and drove out of my life forever...

Grabbing Dale's ermine coat by the sleeve, I pulled her back. Both she and Roy cordially autographed my book, and I kept the pen as a keepsake that nobody--but nobody--could ever use.

Back home that night, I could not sleep. I had actually seen and spoken to ROY ROGERS!

Years later, my five-year-old child would see him too, feel the same enchantment I had felt, and cherish the same autograph I had cherished.

I imagine (and expect) the legend will live on for many more generations to come. Roy Rogers will always represent everything that is pure and wholesome. He will always bring to remembrance a more innocent time when children did not see blaring, realistic scenes of gore and violence, and when they could lie down at night, not to nightmares, but to pleasant dreams of when Good always won.

Sadly, as we see Roy Rogers, the legend, ride quietly off into the sunset, we see no one ready to take his place. We can, however, still hear him say, "Goodbye, good luck, and may the Good Lord take a likin' to ya."

That was Roy Rogers to an eleven-year-old girl. That is Roy Rogers today. My Hero. Mr. Knight in Shining Armor. Then, now, and...always...

MAGNET MESSAGE:

Return us, Dear Father, to a time of decency and righteousness so that once again, our nation may be exalted. In Jesus' name, Amen.

"Righteousness exalteth a nation...." Proverbs 14:34

43. Betty Lou, Eyelashes, and Me

Every other Sunday, my best friend, Betty Lou, would come home with me from church. The other Sunday, I would go home with her. She was as close as a sister to me. She brought her little bag to church and slipped it under our pew and leaning over whispered, "I brought it!" We clasped our hands over our mouths, looked to see if anyone was listening, and then giggled our faces off about "it"!

As soon as church was over, we beelined it to the car. When Sunday dinner had been consumed and we had washed the dishes, we changed out of our "Sunday clothes" and into our "play clothes" to play. We rode our bikes, twirled our batons, played hopscotch, and made ourselves "Miss America" banners, strutting around in our swimming suits as if we had just been crowned with that glorious title, at the same time clomping down the driveway in high heels four sizes too large! We roller-skated, jumped rope, and a million other things.

When 3:00 came around, though, it was time for The Shadow radio show. Lamont Cranston became invisible to catch the crooks, and he would utter those now-famous words: "Who knows what evil lurks in the hearts of men? The Shadow knows--Hehahaheha," and he laughed that laugh that chilled us to the bone.

When The Shadow went off the air, Betty Lou would get

the little sack and retrieve "it." "It" was her mother's eyelash curler! For some unknown reason, this little gadget held a deep fascination to two little girls. We curled our lashes until they stuck straight up to our brows. We waited until just before time to go back to evening worship to plaster our lashes with Vaseline in order to hold them up there where they would stay. Once back in our pew, we batted our eyes and rolled them around to see if anyone was looking. Betty Lou would have put the little device back in her little brown bag and once she got home, she would slip it back in her mother's drawer so that we could use it again the next week when I went home with her. We really thought we were getting by with something.

Betty Lou and I remained best friends through college years until we went separate ways and eventually lost contact. We had first met when we were six years old, and she remained for many years a precious and treasured friend. We laughed together about the "craziest things" that were so simple, but gave us such joy.

Sundays have many happy memories for me, and Betty Lou is one of them.

MAGNET MESSAGE:

Thank you, God for the gift of friends. No one can have too many, for they soften the blows of life, and although they know us, they still love us. In Jesus' name, Amen

"A friend loves at all times." Proverbs 17:17

44. As Bright and As Pure As the Driven Snow

W hat daughter does not want to be the apple of her father's eye? To be complimented and made to feel
loved and feminine is the bliss of being a girl.

When autograph books were the "in" thing, imagine my joy
when I received my very own 4x5 brown leather-bound autograph book when I was in the sixth grade. This was the chance
we had wanted--to gather the thoughts of all our friends.

We brought our books to school and passed them around
for each friend to write something special, and then we agreed
to take them home for our fathers to sign. The next day was a
cold, snowy day at Hawthorne School in Oklahoma City, and
recess was called off, so we gathered around to read aloud each
other's messages and to compare what our fathers had written.

As I listened to the girls read what their fathers had writ-
ten--"My darling daughter," "My little Baby-Pie," "My gorgeous
little doll"-- I died of embarrassment. I choked on what MY
daddy had written to me, his second daughter and next-to-
oldest child: "Dear Belle:" (he always called me that, but did he
have to write it for the whole world to see?) "I hope you will
always be as bright and as pure as the driven snow. Love, Daddy."

For what seemed like an eternity, the girls said not one word. Finally, one of the girls broke the silence and said breathlessly and quietly, "I wish my daddy had said that to me."

I did not understand--not then and not for many years. Later, I realized that Daddy, in that one short, poetic sentence, summed up all the hopes and dreams he had for me. I would learn later on that his fondest wish and dream for all four of his girls was that they would be as "bright and pure" as their mother.

That little book today remains my most cherished treasure.

MAGNET MESSAGE:

Give us the pure heart of an innocent child that the world may see You in us. In Jesus' name, Amen.

"Blessed are the pure in heart for they shall see God." Matthew 5:8

45. "I'm 'that way'"

"I have something to tell all of you after supper tonight." My mother's words were somber and reflective, but she had a twinkle in her eyes and the corners of her mouth kept turning up to reveal the excitement she obviously felt. I could hardly wait to hear what it was. We ate supper, cleared the table, and my sister and I did the dishes, faster than we ever had. No fuss this time about why I always dumped plates with food still on them in her dishwater.

Then we gathered in the living room and Mother had us all sit down. "I want to tell you," she began, "I'm that way, [she would never say the word "pregnant"] so in November, you three can expect a new baby brother or sister. I really do not want you to tell anyone or even discuss it. It is our family's business."

How in the world could she expect me to keep such a wonderful thing a secret? I was just eleven years old and I would not-- could not--keep my mouth shut about something this exciting! We all three squealed in unison: "I get to take care of it!" An argument followed over which one of us would get to help with it. My brother ended up bawling about it the way he always did about everything. He was seven and my sister was thirteen. I did not understand why such a marvelous event should be kept a secret.

Mother continued. "There are many people who will think we have too many children already or that I am too old, and will not understand that all of you were wanted and planned."

That sure sounded strange to me. What did she mean? That some people didn't want the babies they have? And how did you plan for one? I just thought they came upon the scene suddenly and surprised everybody, just like Mother was doing at this moment.

Who in the world, I thought, wouldn't want a baby? And who in the world could keep such a secret? Certainly not me! The next day, I went to school and told just everybody!

The months to follow passed slowly, but finally, on November 17, 1948, a baby girl arrived. When Mother was in labor, Daddy said she told the doctor her "next baby" would also be a girl. "Never in the thirty-five years I have delivered babies," the doctor told Daddy, "have I had a mother while in labor talk about her next baby!"

Our baby sister went for a while without a name. Mother and Daddy could not agree on the best name for her. Daddy wanted to name her Suzy Quail (it was quail season, and he was an avid hunter) and call her Suzy Q. Mother wouldn't hear of it. I felt what they came up with was even worse. Mother's nickname was Polly (short for Pauline), and Daddy's nickname was Pat, so they decided on Polly Pat. I was mortified. I hated it.

I refused to say it and did not even tell anyone because I was ashamed of it. At school, all the kids kept asking me if my sister had a name yet. I finally had to say it. I mumbled it hoping they wouldn't ask again. They did. They laughed, too, just like I knew they would.

That spring, Mother brought the baby to school. What a glorious day for me! She walked in carrying Polly Pat and had dressed her in a fluffy yellow frock, her black hair and black eyes shining, her adorable papoose (Indian heritage showing) face framed in a yellow lace bonnet. I cannot remember ever having had a prouder moment! When Mother entered the room with this--the most beautiful baby I had ever seen! --I stood and announced loud and clear: "THIS IS MY MOTHER AND THIS IS POLLY PAT, MY NEW BABY SISTER!" I was never again ashamed of her name. It seemed to fit the cuddly, lovable little doll that I wished were my own.

Then the trouble began. My older sister, Sally, took over. She wouldn't let me hold, feed, or bathe Polly Pat; said she was HERS. She wouldn't ever share. Bob, our little brother didn't even get to help at all unless it was to run get things for her.

As I recalled Mother's announcement about Polly Pat, I began to secretly pray for her to make another one like it. It was obvious that Sister (which is what I always called Sally) was never going to share. If my prayers were to be answered, then another baby sister would be mine. I would show Sister a thing or two, I'd just "go over her head" and pray. Besides, Mother had said her "next baby would be a girl." Hadn't the doctor told Daddy she said that?

I would just wait....and pray...

MAGNET MESSAGE:

Thank you, God, for blessing our lives with precious children. They are the greatest gifts anyone can receive. Help us to "train them in the way they should go." In Jesus' name, Amen.

"As arrows are in the hand of a mighty man; so are the children of thy youth. Happy is the man who has his quiver full of them...."
Psalm 127:4-5

46. *"I'm 'that way'—again"*

Daddy sat at his desk working on a blueprint of the next house he would build, Mother sat mending clothes, and we children were listening to Amos 'N Andy on the radio. Quietly, Mother put aside her mending, stood up, and turned off the radio. Our outcries of protest were soon squelched when she said, "Hush, I have something to tell you."

My heart pounded! I saw the same look on her face I had seen three years before when she had said to all of us "I'm 'that way'" and had given us our adorable little "papoose" look-alike sister named Polly Pat.

"I'm 'that way' again," she began as I tried to slow my racing heart! "Your daddy and I planned for all of you, and this one is no exception. Because I am almost forty, people will say I am too old and don't know when to quit. For this reason, I must ask all of you not to jabber about it to others. It just isn't something I want people to talk about. It is our business."

I glanced over toward Daddy and caught him peering over the top of his $1.00 TG&Y magnifying glasses. His eyes twinkled, and the corners of his mouth twitched to keep from bursting out in laughter. After all, he was almost forty-five!

I thought I just couldn't wait another six months, and I knew I could not keep this secret any better than I kept the last one. Three years did not make a dent on my maturity. I didn't

understand any more now than I did then. By now I was fourteen so I decided to tell only my closest friends. Could I help it there were so many of them?

Since I had secretly been praying for another baby sister so I would have one to take care of as my own, I wasn't too surprised at the announcement. I just thought it took 'way too long to come about. I was afraid I would grow up and miss the chance.

My older sister had taken charge of Polly Pat. I would take charge of this one. This was clearly an answer to my prayers, and I had no doubts that it would be anything other than a girl. But Bob wanted a brother.

The next six months seemed to drag, but finally the big moment came. Daddy called from the hospital that night on January 17, 1952, as we sat by the phone waiting. Bob answered it. Daddy said, "Well, Bob, it's another dad-blamed girl!" and Bob threw the telephone, causing the spring-cord on it to bounce back and strike the lamp, breaking it. He threw himself onto the couch sobbing. My only thought was: at last, a baby for me! My prayers had been answered!

As the weeks and months turned into years, I don't recall ever being so completely happy! We four girls went everywhere together. I got to bathe, dress, feed and rock my live doll and I loved every minute of it. Sister (Sally, my older sister) took Polly Pat, and I took Ellen Sue and dressed alike, we would go to downtown Oklahoma City and have pictures made, shop, and mostly just show off our living, breathing, beautiful baby dolls. Once when we were all (including Mother) in John A. Brown's Department Store, a group of women kept staring and whispering about us.

Mother asked them if something was wrong. "Well, we were just noticing those two small children. The teen-aged girls are too young to be their mother and you are too old. We were just wondering whose children they are?"

The years seemed to fly too fast, and as we two older girls gradually left for college, things began to change. Darling babies grow up, a disappointed little brother mends his broken heart, and parents age. But memories build to last a lifetime.

Finally, Mother said she had to admit her age, and it was with a genuine sense of sadness that we heard her say, "I will never be 'that way' again."

MAGNET MESSAGE:

Thank you for wonderful memories of those darling babies You sent our family. May we never forget that children are a gift and blessing from You. In Jesus' name, Amen.

"And a little child shall lead them." Isaiah 11:6

47. From the Silken Throat of a Tiny Bird

A most unusual little bird, "Lemon Drop" was a beautiful canary. She had been given to us when our baby sister was one year old, and her cage stood just beside the baby's crib. Baby Ellen was fascinated with the petite, lemon-colored creature. She would stand for long periods of time at the end of her crib, facing Lemon Drop, and Lemon Drop seemed to perform for her as the baby giggled and bounced around in her crib.

Mother noticed one day that when the water ran in the sink or tub, Lemon Drop would sing.... And SING! When the faucet was opened up full force, Lemon Drop would "open up her throat" full force, and the trill would pierce the air, only to stop abruptly when the water was shut off.

It didn't matter if we were running dishwater, bath water, the shower, even flushing the stool, if Lemon Drop heard running water, she sang! We never realized how much water we were using until we got that bird! It became a game to us children. If we were in trouble and Mother began one of her lengthy lectures that we had heard one hundred times, one of us would sneak into the bathroom and turn on the water faucet. Lemon Drop's shrill song would drown out Mother's lecture, and that seemed a more respectful way to ignore her than covering our ears as we usually did when lecture number one hundred and one began.

"Who turned on that water?" Mother demanded when Lemon Drop cut loose. We looked around at each other and burst out laughing. It was sometimes very hard for Mother to stay mad at us.

One morning, Mother was having an unusually bad day when the washing machine broke, the commode overflowed, and the water heater sprung a leak, all simultaneously, it seemed. Not only that, but my sister had turned on the faucet to make Lemon Drop sing and had forgotten to turn it off. It was running over on the countertop and onto the floor.

With all of these "water sounds," Lemon Drop worked overtime on her operatic abilities, and in utter frustration, Mother exclaimed, "I'm going to get a stopper and put in that bird's mouth, so help me!"

Baby Ellen, by then two years old, disappeared into the bathroom and came out carrying something in her tiny fist. Timidly, and almost teary, she handed an object to Mother. When Mother looked at it, she saw that Baby Ellen had placed the bathtub drain STOPPER quietly in her hand.

No matter how dismal a day could get, when we were children, never did it stay that way for long. There was always something to laugh about and lift us up, be it the antics of our little sisters, the constant clowning of our cats, the chatter of our little brother, or even the shrill songs of a loudmouth bird!

When Lemon Drop wasn't singing, she was hanging upside down or turning her head all the way around to peer directly into our faces with her adorable inquisitive look. She could melt the coldest heart and cause anyone who never cracked a grin, to

dissolve into laughter.

Many pets resided at our home during those years, and Lemon Drop enjoyed a long life even though she lived with many cats. I could never deny the lessons these lovable creatures taught us. What a blessing little ole Lemon Drop was in such a small package. She taught five children that something as simple as the sound of running water could produce a "joyful noise" that filled out home with happiness and cheer.

It was hard to believe that so much of that sweetness, joy, and contentment could come from the silken throat of a tiny bird!

MAGNET MESSAGE:

Give us an unending appreciation for all of Your creatures, dear God. Taking time to enjoy and look for the countless blessings they can give us makes us the recipients of one of life's greatest blessings. In Jesus' name, Amen.

"There be four things which are little upon the earth, but they are exceeding wise: the ants are a people not strong, yet they prepare their meat in the summer, the conies are but a feeble folk, yet make they their houses in the rocks; the locusts have no king, yet they go forth all of them by bands; the spider takes hold with her hands and is in kings' palaces..."

Proverbs 30:24-28

48. Nylon Hose and Fancy Garter Belts

I will never forget my first pair of nylon hose. The war over, nylon was once again plentiful, and I thought the silky sheerness of a pair of nylon hose was the most beautiful thing I had ever seen. Complete with a seam up the back, stockings had to be fastened to little elasticized tabs, which hung from a lace-covered undergarment called a garter belt.

The most difficult thing about a thirteen-year-old wearing stockings was trying to keep the seams straight. The seam ran slap-dab up the back of the legs, and the least movement in the wrong direction could send the seams twisting around until sometimes they appeared on the front of the leg! There was nothing--and I mean nothing--more unlady-like than to see a girl with crooked seams, or worse yet, a runner.

It was the Christmas just after I turned thirteen, and we were at our grandparents' home in Crandall, Texas. Mother always insisted when we visited her parents that we "dress for the occasion," and that particular year was my first time to get to wear nylon hose. I must have been a comical sight. I had to disappear every few minutes to go into the bathroom to "adjust things," all while my ten-year-old cousin constantly reminded me in obvious jealousy, "You're not old enough to wear those." She made me so mad. Here I was trying to act so grown up, and

she and those crooked seams just wouldn't let me. And as if that wasn't bad enough, the hose got baggy, and the wrinkles looked even worse.

I remember when we gathered around the table--all fifty or so of us--and the prayer began, I started to squirm. The garter belt was too large and was slipping down, the hose seam was twisted, and the bags around my ankles were overlapping. During the prayer, I thought while everybody had their heads bowed and eyes closed, I could make a necessary "adjustment" on the situation. With my own head bowed, I proceeded to raise my skirt to straighten the seams, and looking up through my eyebrows without raising my head, I saw my mischievous cousin with her hand over her mouth, and I heard her muffled giggle burst out into full-fledged laughter. Of course, the prayer stopped, and everybody, in stony silence, glared at the little girl, and then, looking over at the cause of the fuss, they saw me. I was standing there with my skirt half hanging above the lop-sided garter belt, the back seams coiled and twisted around to the front of my legs, and the wrinkles hanging around my ankles like The Saggy Baggy Elephant! Everyone broke into laughter!

I was mortified! I had never thought for one moment that "being a woman" would bring such embarrassment. I had never seen anyone else have these problems. Why me? I just knew that it hadn't been as much fun as I had imagined it would be, and I ran from the room in humiliation.

The family went on with the meal, and Mother came to the bathroom to console me. It was a long time before I came out, but Mother assured me that I would live through it and "someday laugh about it."

I didn't believe that for one minute. I wanted to die. But

Mother was right. I did live through it and I did laugh about it. In fact, it became the annual Christmas tradition at my grandparents' house from then on to laugh about "the time Molly Lou almost lost her hose during the prayer."

You just had to develop a sense of humor in our family if you expected to survive!

MAGNET MESSAGE:

Give us a humble spirit, O God, one that is truly void of pride and vanity, as we look to You for our spirituality and forgiveness. In Jesus' name, Amen.

"Pride goeth before destruction, and a haughty spirit before a fall." Proverbs 16:18

49. *The Graduation Dress*

Teenagers of the 1950's were not all that different from the teens of today. It often took great courage and self-confidence--even as it does today--to be an individual of one's own choosing, and not follow the crowd, whether it be in something as simple as the way you dressed, or something as complicated as practicing, in the midst of scoffers, the convictions in which you strongly believed.

So as a teen of the '50's, I was no different. One of Mother's favorite lectures was on the subject of "being true to yourself," and she constantly emphasized that it did not hurt to be an individual with different tastes from the majority, and that we could do it! Sometimes it was extremely hard to "go against the current," even though our hearts told us to do so.

Back then, junior high was the seventh, eighth, and ninth grades. High school was tenth, eleventh, and twelfth. When one finished the ninth grade, a graduation ceremony was held equivalent to the twelfth grade graduation, minus, of course, the caps and gowns. Commencement speakers were elected, pretty dresses were bought, and the gifts rolled in. It was almost as exciting as that final graduation from high school.

Toward the end of my ninth grade with commencement day approaching, our class met to elect the commencement speakers. I was elated and proud to be elected one of the two girls selected for that honor. As the girls in the class all began to talk about their graduation dresses, I realized that almost everybody would be wearing white, with a few choosing pastels of pink or blue. I did not want to be like everybody else, but felt I had no choice, and even if I did, could I do it?

Mother took the ball and ran with it. She engaged a seamstress to make my dress. I picked out the pattern, but I was not ready for the color of the fabric she suggested. It was bright orange--the color of a sunset! Absolutely beautiful...but for graduation? I just couldn't see it. No way was I going to be THAT different. I agreed with Mother that it was perfectly gorgeous, but ORANGE ME in a sea of white and pastels! I would stand out too much! "That's all right," Mother said, "You should stand out, you're the speaker."

I finally agreed to her idea. The dress was organdy with puffed sleeves, the gathered yoke attached to a high waistband that was in turn, attached to a full, gathered skirt, under which I was to wear those mountains of starched petticoats. Mother purchased a brown velvet ribbon that tied around my waist and topped it with a peach-colored rose. I had to admit it was truly the prettiest dress I had ever seen, but I dreaded the day I would wear it.

At school, as the dresses were the talk of every day, I was often asked about mine. When I said--with all of the courage I could muster, and covering my uneasiness--, "Oh, it is as beautiful as a sunrise--bright orange!" the girls gasped. "Orange? For graduation?" Then they made faces. I just pretended that they were the ones out of step and went on my way.Little by little, they began to think maybe pastels were not so great after all.

The big day arrived. As "Pomp and Circumstance" began

and we started to file in, I saw my baby sister in her stroller in the aisle, beside Mother's seat. My other little sister was bouncing around on her seat next to Daddy, and I momentarily forgot about the ORANGE DRESS. I suddenly just felt like the luckiest girl in the whole world!

Then I saw it! The stage where I was to sit and the podium where I was to stand were beautifully decorated with flowers and greenery. I could not believe my eyes! The stage was literally covered with gladiolus and they were bright orange! It seems the entire class saw it at the same time. A wave of "ooohh" went through the line.

"No wonder Molly chose orange," they murmured. "It blends." I just smiled and made my way up to the stage. It worked out so well that people thought I had color-coodinated my dress for the occasion, but the secret was that I had not. I wondered if Mother had known...I was never to find out.

MAGNET MESSAGE:

Help us, Dear God, to give to our children the courage and self discipline to be true to themselves, regardless of the actions of others. In Jesus' name, Amen.

"Rejoice in the Lord always, I will say it again: Rejoice!"
Philippians 4:4

50. The Blizzard

I had built for myself quite a waiting list as a baby sitter when I was a teenager, adding new names to it almost daily. On a freezing night in December 1951, when Mother was eight months pregnant, I was asked to baby-sit for one of my new clients who lived in adjacent North Creston Hills. Mother always tried to screen the families for whom we baby sat, but she agreed to this one on the recommendation of a friend---against her better judgment, she would later tell me.

The Browns were a military family and when Lieutenant Brown picked me up to take me to their home, he told Mother it would probably be "rather late," as they were going to go to one of his "military parties."

I had no idea just how late "rather late" was, until a very intoxicated Mr. Brown called saying it would probably be "4:00, or maybe 5:00 am" before they would be home.

My first impulse as a "child" was to call Mother because I was scared. Who would take me home? My second impulse as an "I-think-I-am-grown-up" kept me from calling her, reassuring myself that I could handle anything. I was fourteen years old.

The night wore on. Mother called and I told her not to worry, but it would be VERY late. I did not say HOW late. A freezing combination of rain, sleet, and snow began to fall, and I peeked outside. The yards and streets in front of the house were

solid sheets of ice. The blizzard was building. And so were my worries.

At 3:30 am., a very inebriated Mr. Brown and a slightly drunk Mrs. Brown came in. I wondered how they had possibly made it home. They must have started back before the worse part of the storm. Even then, I wondered how they had maneuvered the car.

Mrs. Brown paid me and Mr. Brown started to the door while I got my coat. I can remember vividly the absolute terror that pierced my heart! He was in no condition to get into a car, much less drive one.

When we walked out to the porch, I saw a snow-covered car parked in the street, and I immediately recognized it as ours.

Inside, my precious mother had wrapped herself in a wool blanket, pregnant and all, to wait for me. She was not about to let me be driven home by a stranger who might be drunk.

I would later learn that she had been sitting there since midnight. As the storm had gotten much worse, she simply bundled herself up and went over to wait for me, thinking perhaps the Browns' party might get out of hand. No doubt, it had. I will never forget the flood of thanksgiving that washed over me when I saw Mother in that car. It was a wonderful feeling of relief!

BUT when I got into the car, I let her know in no uncertain terms that I thought she had treated me like a child and how humiliated I was.

Mother did not say a word. Just started the car, and we crawled carefully home on the ice, slipping and sliding all of the way. When we finally got there, this grateful teen fell into bed, without a word of appreciation.

Four weeks later, my baby sister was born.

Mother was a strong woman of courage and principles. If she was hurt by teen-age rebellion, I was never to know it. Her strength of character and purpose in life lay in her ability to always do what was right. Her family was her first and foremost love, and that involved making decisions for us that we were not yet mature enough to make for ourselves.

All of my life when a blizzard hits, I am immediately taken back to that cold December night when my mother curled under a blanket in the freezing night, and waited for me. And waited. . . .and waited. . .

MAGNET MESSAGE:

Let us always remember to give flowers to the living, dear Father, while they are with us to enjoy their beauty and depth of meaning. Parents like ours are especially deserving of this honor. Give us time to bestow it. In Jesus' name, Amen.

"Her children rise up and call her blessed." Proverbs 31:28

51. Slumber(less) Parties

As spring arrived in full blossom and warm days arrived toward the end of school of the school year when I was a teen, my sister and I often hosted outdoor slumber parties. We each invited six of our best friends to come and be a part of the fun.

School usually didn't end until around the first of June every year, so there were plenty of nice weekends for our parties.

We asked each girl to bring a cot and bedding; during lunch at school, we took a piece of paper and drew our sleeping arrangement diagrams. My sister's half of the back yard was on the west side, my half was the east. The little diagrams we drew up showed how the cots were to be placed so that all of our heads would be together. This was so all of the storytelling, gossip, and giggles could be shared equally, and no one would be left out.

All of the girls had better be a friend to cats also, because when morning came, one of my many felines would be curled up on the end of each cot.

Since we were not allowed to wear jeans to school--or any kind of pants, for that matter--the girls would have to go home after school to change into their jeans.

Mother had supper ready for us by the time all the girls got there and we were "set up." She served it on the backyard picnic table, and she had all kinds of goodies whipped up for "midnight snacks."

We thought we had so much to do and so little time to do it. Important things like forming a conga line and bunny-hopping around the neighborhood, going on a scavenger hunt, seeing who could jump the farthest distance from a moving swing, and who could tell the scariest story. We "slept" in our jeans, but the sleeping bags helped protect us against the heavy dew that always appeared in the early morning hours.

But the most fun of all came when we all got zipped up in our sleeping bags, got our flashlights, and waited for "the rocks!"

We always made sure that word got around school that "the Rogers sisters are having a slumber party tonight." That was the most fun of all because it brought out ornery boys who would plunk us with rocks and hit the metal garbage cans with them, trying to scare us. Our parents' bedroom was at the back of the house, and their window was always open. They were in a perfect spot to keep a watchful eye on everything, and they did just that!

When the spray of gravel bits hit our cots, we squealed and screamed like young girls do, loving every minute of it. We pretended to be terrified, much to the boys' delight. We grabbed our flashlights and aimed the beam of light toward the direction of the noises. With a little help from Mother, who spoke out the window with "Enough is enough, boys," they would quickly scurry away!

The rest of the evening, between trips to the trays of candies, popcorn, colas, nuts, and crackers and cheeses on the picnic table, we listened to 45-rpm records on the phonograph we had situated in the window. Eddie Fisher, Perry Como, Dean Martin, Nat King Cole, and Tony Bennett singing our favorites--Tell Me Why, No Other Love, Everybody Loves Somebody, Pretend, and Rags to Riches--crooned to us all through the night. Even as we giggled, shared dreams that young girls dream, and told ghost stories, the songs on the records drifted endlessly through the night air. We never grew tired of playing the same songs over and over. (I wonder how Mother and Daddy slept?)

Bright and early Saturday morning, Mother popped out the back door with homemade cinnamon rolls, hot chocolate, scrambled eggs, bacon, and juice for the sleepy-eyed, now run-down group.

After breakfast, the girls' mothers picked them up, they went home, changed clothes, and we regrouped for a trip downtown for shopping and a matinee movie. There were 14 tired girls, but when we got home--for my sister and me--there were our usual Saturday chores awaiting us.

Losing sleep was no excuse for not doing our Saturday afternoon routine, including working our Bible lessons, "for the Lord's Day," Mother would say. She never allowed us to miss getting our Bible worksheets done, no matter how "tired" we were.

My sister and I had many slumber parties during our teen years, and they left us with happy, pleasant memories of a time in young lives when things were as they should be. Once in awhile, even today, I run into former classmates from those years, and they always tell me, "I still remember those fun slumber(less) parties you used to have!"

MAGNET MESSAGE:

Help us, Dear God, to realize that memories are precious possessions that time can never destroy. We are grateful for them. While we do not want to live in the past, we surely do like to visit there, and often!In Jesus' name, Amen.

"A gentle tongue is a tree of life, but perverseness in it breaks the spirit." Proverbs 15:4

52. Mohawk!

There seems to be a popular theory that all little girls who have brothers learn very early to adopt an easy, bantering manner toward members of the opposite sex. If it were our little brother from which you expected to learn that, you would be sadly misled. He was not, by any stretch of the imagination, your "average little brother." You would never dare to put into practice what you had learned from him because he was unlike any other person of the male persuasion.

He changed on a daily, minute-by-minute basis. Just as you thought you had him figured out, he changed the rules. He could make you laugh without even intending to. A totally charming and darling little boy.

The barbershop our daddy and brother used was in our neighborhood, and within walking distance from our house. One Saturday, Bob went to get his hair cut. As soon as he had climbed into the barber chair, Mother got a call from the barber.

"Your son wants a special cut today. Is that all right with you?" the barber asked. Mother replied, "Of course, he may wear it however he chooses."

There was nothing to be concerned about; there were only a few ways a fellow would wear his hair back then: flat-top, duck tail or "old man" style, parted on the side, greased, and taper-cut up the back. None of us were prepared for what walked into our living room door that afternoon! Bob had gotten a Mohawk haircut! Mother didn't know whether to laugh or cry. His head looked like an eight-ball except for the thick strip of hair sticking straight up right down the middle of his noggin.

The next morning when we walked into church services, everything was disrupted because the song leader got so tickled, he couldn't lead the singing. I was embarrassed. We were to leave for church camp right after worship, and I decided I didn't want anyone to know that this nutty-looking kid with a strip down the middle of his head was kin to me.

This was the same little brother who at age five, had picked up his little rubber dagger, turned over a crate in the back yard, crawled up on it, and proclaimed as loudly as he could scream: "Goodbye, cruel world, I now commit adultery!" and plunged the little rubber dagger into his chest as he tumbled off the crate and onto the ground in agonizing "pain" of suicide.

This was the same little brother who, years later, would paint the words, "The Neckin' Wreck" on the fender of his first car and would be asked by a church member to park it somewhere other than the church parking lot. "It sets a bad example," he was told.

Now this same little brother thought he would go to church camp with a peeled head and embarrass me some more! I would just make sure that no one ever knew I was his sister.

All that week of camp, the name Mohawk kept popping up. No one even knew his real name .The stories were endless:

Mohawk got thrown into the lake for reading the preacher's love letters out loud over his shoulder as he wrote to his fiancée. (It was that haircut; I was sure of it!)

Mohawk got KP for locking the preachers in the camp store and not letting them out. (That haircut again; it brings out the worst in this little guy.)

Mohawk got grounded for grabbing four hamburgers off the platter and taking a bite out of each one before the prayer. (That stupid haircut, I just knew it.)

It was Mohawk, Mohawk, Mohawk--all week, every day! I began to feel sorry for him. He put frogs where frogs did not belong, he tied knots in his sheets and hung them out his window, and the wind whipped them until they came loose and blew away, and he sneaked into the canteen after hours for snacks.

One morning during Bible class, which we held outside under the trees, I heard him discussed so much I began to cry. After all, he was still my little brother. I stayed behind after the class dismissed so I could cry privately. The teacher, missing me, returned, and asked me why I was crying. "It's Mohawk," I sobbed. "He's my brother, and everybody is so mean to him!" I will never forget her total shock and amazement at that revelation. It wasn't long until the entire camp knew that "Mohawk is Molly's brother!" Finally, the miserable week was over and thankfully, Bob's hair began to grow out, and once again, his name was Bob. No one ever again expected me to have an advantage in knowing the ways of the male species just because I had a brother. No, sir, my little brother had been Mohawk, and he was certainly no example from which to learn any consistent male behavioral patterns!

MAGNET MESSAGE:

Give us a sense of humor. Struggling through life without it can multiply sorrows. In Jesus' name, Amen.

"A merry heart does as much good as a medicine." Proverbs 17:22

53. *First Love*

It is said that of all the five senses, the sense of smell is the one to which the heart most readily responds to memories. When I was a young girl, the warm summer evenings soaked up the sweet scent of the lilac bush growing outside my bedroom window and released it through the gentle breeze over and over again.

The bush was so plush that it partly covered our front porch and it was underneath that umbrella of loveliness that I said good night to "First Love".

Our evening walks, our bicycle rides, the shared sodas in the local drug store, the strolls down the school hall with him carrying my books, the gaudy ring on the chain around my neck, and the bulky, heavy letter jacket that swallowed my then-petite frame, are all blissful memories of "First Love." But the dearest memories of all flood my mind when lilacs are in bloom. Because it was under the lilac bush that I slipped him poems scented with his favorite perfume, and it was under the lilac bush that we had our most endearing discussions about life and where we were headed.

Dates to go skating, to the movies, to play miniature golf, and to the ice cream parlor, all ended romantically under that beautiful lilac bush. That ever-flashing porch light would sometimes interrupt the magic of the evening. I remember once when "First Love" climbed up and removed the bulb.

It somehow found its way back into the socket, and deep down, I really had appreciated the "safety" it provided, and the assurance that someone inside cared enough to wait up for me.

"First Love" was pure, innocent, and full of anticipation. It was unspoiled, unpretentious, and completely honest. It began long before the lilac bush was planted.

It was in kindergarten when he first "claimed" me and picked up those big, fat crayons for me when I dropped them on the floor. He always helped me get on my boots when it rained and he walked me home. We attended church together, the same elementary school and high school. We grew up in the same neighborhood and we were friends.

As time changed things, somewhere down the line, our lives took different directions, and contact with "First Love" was lost.

The lilac bush has long since died, the pressed flowers and the photographs in the treasured scrapbook have faded and crumbled with time. It is a sweet memory to look at them, but a whiff of lilac perfume will put me once again into my girlhood home, under the flowering lilac bush, and my heart will stir softly within me as I recall my "First Love."

 MAGNET MESSAGE:

Never let us dwell too long in the past, dear Father, lest we miss the beauty and blessings of today. Help us to realize that early-in-life experiences of "First Love" go into the shaping and molding of our character as an adult. In Jesus' name, Amen.

"But he that shall endure to the end shall be saved." Matt. 24:13

54. Fabulous Fifties Fashions

A nthony's had them for one dollar each. They came in all sizes. And the more you could "stand" to wear, the better. Of course, I had to wear fifteen! But after all, they were only one layer of netting sewed in tiers, and it took that many to make a soft circular skirt stand out to get that "just right" look.

I was a teenager, and fluffy petticoats were very popular. Some of the girls preferred the "horse-hair" petticoats, but I thought they were too "scratchy." Besides, the net ones, when fifteen were stacked together, made a prettier, softer silhouette, I thought.

The thickness of that many rows of elastic around my waist quite often left what I thought would be a permanent crease in my waistline. But all of us at that time thought it was worth it, because we could cinch up a twenty-four inch waist into a twenty-two inch waist with those heavy elastic stretch belts. Pull on a soft blouse, float a full skirt over the petticoats, tuck in the blouse, hook the stretch belt over the bulky waist, sweep the hair up into a ponytail, top it with a ribbon, and finish off the look with a pair of white satin ballerina slippers. And a "fifties teen-age girl" was ready for school, a date, or church.

If a girl chose the heavier petticoats that required wearing only one, the starching process could take quite a while. To stand out at maximum width, they were "sugar-starched" and spread out on the lawn to dry in full circle. Woe to the mother who hung them on the line! They dried too flat. Only spread on the grass could they dry to recognize their "full" potential. I can remember riding in a car and being unable to see through the windshield...because of the height of my petticoats billowing up in front of me! To sugar-starch them, we mixed sugar and water and dipped the slips into the solution before spreading them to dry. This didn't always work too well, though, because on a hot, muggy Oklahoma day, legs got pretty sticky, and no one enjoyed feeling like they were sitting in a syrup bucket!

Sugar water didn't end with petticoat starching. It also ended up on our hair for setting. We combed the sugar water through the hair like a setting gel, and often rolled it on orange juice cans to get the long, bouncy curls. It held the hair in place, too--until humidity took over. Then the sugar was not only sticky and gooey, but our heads attracted insects as well. And so much for another teen fad. . .

The lipstick of the day was Revlon's Pink Queen, and the perfume was Blue Waltz (ugh). The makeup had to be Revlon's Touch & Glow, usually "creamy ivory," unless you were very dark.

We washed our hair every night, often with Joy Detergent to keep down the oil, and we had bows to match every set of clothes. The bow clipped in above the curls or topped a pony-tail. Our skirts and sweaters during the winter months were "dyed to match," and at the neck of our sweaters, we tied a small silk scarf in a square knot, snapped a detachable collar in place, or tied on a tiny velvet bow.

Long straight skirts were very popular with slits in the back to allow us to walk. The skirts lacked one inch touching the tops of our bobby sox, and only when the slit opened was there a peek at the leg. Our cheerleaders wore uniforms that were also that length, and they were not allowed to turn flips or do jumps that exposed their legs above the knees.

Sometimes. . . I wish for them back. . .those fabulous fifties fashions!

MAGNET MESSAGE:

Give us a sense of humor, Dear Father, and a cheerful heart that we may ever see the joy in praising You and living for You. In Jesus' name, Amen.

"Pleasant words are like a honeycomb, sweetness to the soul and health to the body." Proverbs 16:24

55. *Mother's Chocolate Chip Cookies*

One of my favorite memories of Mother is of her standing in front of the "dough board" making chocolate chip cookies. Daddy built a little board into the cabinet that pulled out and gave her the extra room she needed to create her delicious confections.

I associate chocolate chip cookies in my memory with one of the greatest lessons in discipline I learned as a teenager. Even today, when I bite into a freshly-made chocolate chip cookie, I think back to a time when I was thirteen years old. It was a Saturday.

The telephone rang, and a boy from school was on the other end. He was the most popular, most handsome boy in school and every girl would die for a chance to have him call her---back then boys did the calling--and I was elated, to say the least. There was one problem, however. His reputation was somewhat questionable, and although I knew this, I still felt a little flattered that he called me.

"Hi, Molly," he began. My heart raced. I recognized his voice. "This is James. How would you like to go swimming with me this afternoon at Black Hawk Park?"

All kinds of thoughts whirled through my mind. Swimming? This has got to be the worst possible thing that could happen to me, I thought. Of course, I could not go swimming with him. . .but I couldn't let him know that; he would think me a child!

I glanced into the kitchen where I could see Mother making those cookies, and the thoughts that raced through my mind were: What if she says, "yes"? What will I do? James was considered the "fastest" guy at school. I was scared. How could I get out of this? "Just a moment, I'll ask my mother if I can go," I told him as all of these thoughts clouded my mind. As I put down the receiver and started toward the kitchen, I think I died over and over again. I remember the walk from the living room to the kitchen seemed an eternity, and there was only a dining room separating them.I would not know what to do if Mother gave me permission. I was not yet confident and mature enough to make my own decisions, and peer pressure was always lurking around every corner. Mother would have to make the decision for me. I was depending on her. But what if she said, "yes"?

"Mother," I said. "It's James Baker. He wants me to go out to Black Hawk Park swimming with him. May I?" I recall it as if it were yesterday how my heart pounded within my chest. I was terrified.

"Of course not. You know better than to even ask," Mother answered confidently, without even looking up from the dough she was making into little balls. Inside, I sighed a sigh of relief. She had never let me down; why had I thought she would now? She loved me and protected me when I did not have the mature confidence to make my own decisions, and I was very grateful for it.

BUT when I returned to the telephone, I picked it up and with all the disgust and hateful tone in my voice I could muster, I said, "No, James, I can't go. Mother won't let me. She never

lets me do anything!"

Did I hurt her feelings? Probably. I will never know. She just did what she knew was right by her children and often told us, "I am not in a popularity contest with your friends." No matter what hurtful things we said to her, she never wavered. It was this consistency and discipline that gave us love and security. It is no wonder that the smell of chocolate chip cookies always brings to my mind once again the memories of this strong and loving mother. But wouldn't it have been nice to tell of this appreciation THEN?

MAGNET MESSAGE:

Thank You for the security You gave us in a faithful, unwavering mother. The lessons she taught us about being strong and true to the beliefs that are right will be carried to eternity. Help us to have her strength of character as we deal with others. In Jesus' name, Amen.

"Let your father and mother be glad; let her who bore you rejoice." Proverbs 23:25

56. *The Skyview*

I remember an especially exciting time for us as children when we were growing up. We watched, with great expectation, a giant movie screen being erected on a large field in northeast Oklahoma City. We had many questions about it and we kept close tabs on its progress. The family took evening drives out to the field to see how far along the construction was. It was a new concept in theaters because one could stay in the car and watch the "picture show." They were calling it the Skyview Theater, and our family was one of hundreds of other families who got in line to "drive in" and watch a movie on opening night.

It was a warm summer night. As the cars lined the road all the way out to the highway, the wait didn't seem long because people hung out of their car windows, visiting and laughing with one another. We knew a lot of the folks because most of them were our neighbors. People back then usually lived in a neighborhood for many years, making it only natural that we would know most of the people in North and South Creston Hills.

That night is a thrilling one in my memory. We pulled the car up on a little mound that angled it just right to be able to see the screen. A little speaker box was hung over the door on the driver's side, and a volume button was all Daddy had to operate to get the sound right into our car. To a child, this was fascinating! There were swings and seesaws on the grass in the front of the screen for children who got restless and wanted to play. A concession stand allowed you to take your food back to your car, or you could sit out on a grassy slope to eat.

When the weather began to get chilly, just before the theater would close for the winter, we loved to go out there as a family with our blankets and pillows. Mother usually popped grocery bags of popcorn and took drinks for us. Sometimes we even wore our p.j.'s, because if it was a double feature, we would get sleepy, so we could just hop right in the bed when we got home.

As I grew into my teen years and began to date, it was confusing to me and I didn't understand why, but there was one place that I was forbidden to go on a date. That place was "The Passion Pit," as drive-in movies were called. Of course, in time, I would come to understand the wisdom of my parents' hard and fast rule of no dates to a drive-in movie. My parents realized by the time I began to date, that drive-ins had evolved into hangouts for wild teenage parties, and although families still frequented them, they had lost some of the flair for family outings that had made them so popular in the beginning.

I began to dread the time a boy might ask me for a date to a drive-in. I rehearsed over and over what I would say. I wanted it to sound like MY decision, not that of my parents. But I didn't understand WHY I couldn't go. I spent many tears over this anxiety and many "mouthings"--as Mother used to call it when I mumbled or "sassed" her over why I had to always be so different from all the other girls. I could see nothing except that I was prevented from having a good time. I did not know of the dangers there.

As I look back and think of all the worry and fear I had of telling a boy that I could not go, the tears I bawled into my pillow late at night--thinking my parents were "mean and didn't understand me,"----I have to admit that I look back in sheer humor. Because the fear and worry that I felt and the tears I shed were all for nothing! Never in my life did a boy ever even ASK me for a date to go to a Drive-in Movie!!

MAGNET MESSAGE:

I'm so very grateful, dear God, for the parents we had. They spent their entire lives consistently working to keep us safe, and our lives pure. That consistency gave our lives stability and made us feel loved, even though we didn't always show it. I just pray that they know now how very much it was appreciated. In Jesus' name, Amen.

"Trust in the Lord with all thine heart...." Proverbs 3:5

57. After-Church Gatherings

W hat cha got cooked up over there?" the teens asked our mother, as they gathered around.

This was no different from any other Sunday night after church when we were teenagers. Our house was the one where the kids always wanted to come.

Mother spent her Sunday afternoons in preparation to welcome--after evening services--about twenty of our friends in our church youth group. Almost every week, she made heavenly fudge, date loaf, or divinity (sometimes all three), cookies, and sandwiches. She stockpiled Par-T-Pak Cola on the back porch, and cases of Coke she purchased for $1.00 a case (of 24), just for these special occasions. I never wondered if she ever got tired, and I never heard her complain about doing it. I just took it all for granted.

Sometimes, when she made her delicious Toll House cookies, I grumbled why we couldn't have "bought cookies" once in a while instead of "always having home-made stuff."

As children, we never tasted a cake mix, or a "mix" of any kind, so when we visited friends we thought to eat a piece of box cake was supposed to be something really special. So just to be like everybody else, we pretended to like it.

When all of the teens from church were gathered in our front room on the floor, Mother bounced in with all of the "goodies" she had made, and the kids were constantly amazed at her unending energy. Sometimes, I think they appreciated her more than her own children did.

When we finished "chowing down," we played all sorts of games. Our favorite was "Mind Teasers." We sometimes tried for hours to figure them out, and if someone got the answer quickly, everybody admired that person very much for being such a "brain."

Immediately after church, when everybody asked Mother if they could come to our house, we gathered up hymnbooks off the racks and carried them to our cars. If it was during the summer, we sat in the back yard and sang.

When we gathered in the back yard and the singing began, it wouldn't be long until neighbors were pulling their lawn chairs out to listen. We weren't even aware that they were there until they began calling out song requests. They kept us busy, many times causing us to sing long into the night.

Sometimes, Mother just split several ice-cold watermelons and we shared them and had a watermelon seed-spitting contest afterwards. In a few weeks, Daddy would be mowing down little watermelon vines that popped up all over our lawn.

Once in awhile, I remember Mother suggesting that we all go to Beverly's Chicken-In-The-Rough after Sunday night services, for one of their huge salads. Those salads were served in giant silver bowls, and four of us could split one for twenty-five cents apiece. I have often wondered if Mother made this suggestion occasionally because she was just plain old tired. If that was ever the reason, we never knew it. It was more important to her to have her children around her with their church friends than to have a house in which we could not live. Although she kept

the house immaculately clean, it was never too clean for us to enjoy--and to enjoy with a lot of other kids, too.

If Mother had a nickel for every time she fixed candy, cookies, cakes, pies, popcorn, hot chocolate, and sandwiches for our church youth group, she would, indeed have been a wealthy woman.

Money isn't always the only indication of wealth, however, and as far as we were concerned, Mother was a wealthy woman and we were the richest children in the world!

MAGNET MESSAGE:

The time to appreciate godly parents is while they are still with us. Help us to realize the brevity of life, so that we may use precious moments allowed us to express this appreciation and thanks. In Jesus' name, Amen

"Even a child is known by his doings, whether his work be pure and whether it be right." Proverbs 20:11

58. Saturday Night Live--50's Style

The maroon-colored plastic radio sat on the nightstand next to our bed when my sister and I were small. She had won it in one of the many contests she entered. Since it was her radio, we always listened to whatever she wanted to hear. But we always agreed on Saturday night programming. It was Saturday Night Live--50's style--and it was called "Your Hit Parade."

After all of our Saturday responsibilities had been finished, we looked forward to retiring with the radio on to listen to our favorite hits of the day. We had certain songs that we liked best and would eagerly listen to see if they were still at the top of the charts. Giselle McKenzie, Snooky Lanson, and Dorothy Collins would head up the star-studded cast of singers, and they would have us humming along with them.

At our high school, we student council officers had gained permission to have a jukebox installed in our cafeteria. It was our responsibility to see that the songs were kept current and that at all times, the top 10 records were on the spindle. It took 25 cents to play five songs, and students kept the most popular songs spinning all through the lunch periods. Sometimes we got requests for special songs someone wanted in the jukebox in order to tell a boyfriend or girlfriend how much they were loved, when only a certain song would do.

I remember very well a song that stayed Number One on

the charts for many weeks. We loved that song. It played over and over on the jukebox at lunch, and each Saturday night, Sister (as I called my older sister) and I would listen to "Your Hit Parade," hopeful that it would still be Number One.

The song was entitled "He," and the opening words were: "He can turn the tide and calm the angry sea; He alone decides who writes a symphony; He lights every star that makes our darkness bright; He keeps watch all through each long and lonely night." Toward the end, it goes, "Though it makes Him sad to see the way we live, He'll always say, 'I forgive.'"

The orchestrated music that accompanied this song was so gorgeous that as it swelled louder and louder in its climactic finale, we would have goose bumps. It was no wonder that it was played at school over and over every day. When it moved to Number Two and finally, off the charts, we missed hearing it. BUT there were always others to come along just as beautiful and with a meaning just as deep as "He."

When television made its big debut in the '50's, "Your Hit Parade" moved to that entertainment mode, as did many other radio programs of the day. Many of those programs succeeded and did even better on TV, while others eventually disappeared. Imagination was lost when you could SEE the program you had heard for so long. Oftentimes, we had visualized them so completely different from what we SAW, that extreme disappointment would set in.

"Your Hit Parade" was one that continued on, even into the TV years, as the singers ACTED out the songs while singing them. There was nothing disappointing there, and Sister and I enjoyed "Your Hit Parade"--Saturday Night Live-'50's style-- every Saturday night for many more years.

MAGNET MESSAGE:

Bring us, dear God, as a nation, back to the values and truths that once made us great. May we turn back to You and reap Your blessings once again. In Jesus' name, Amen.

"Blessed is the nation whose God is the Lord." Psalm 33:12

59. The Frog in Mother's Throat

A ahem!" was the first warning! Two or more to follow meant big trouble, and the sound would increase in volume. If a second eruption was necessary, what we children called the "turtle stretch" followed it.

The sound was the frog in Mother's throat, and it would lodge there any time we misbehaved in church or were late getting to the pew "with our name on it."

The "turtle stretch" was when Mother would grip the back of the pew in front of her, lean forward, and crane her neck to see what was going on up front, much like a turtle stretching out of its shell. If she could not control the problem with the frog in her throat, or the frog-plus-the-stretch, we might see her get up and walk to the front of the church and park herself right square behind us! How humiliating! Why....it was enough to make a young girl behave, if for no other reason.

The most horrifying moment of my teen years came on one such night at Sunday evening services when I was fifteen years old.

When you are fifteen, nothing is more important than looking just right. My best friend and I were in the restroom primping. Every hair on our heads had to be perfect. Somehow, our hairdos were not cooperating. As we continued to comb and brush our hair into place, we heard the first verse of a hymn beginning.

"Linda! I said, "It's started. What will we do?" Panic set in as we discussed our options.

"Well...we could just stay in here," Linda said.

"I'd get killed," I said.

"Well, maybe we could fake a stomach ache," she answered.

"I'd get killed worse."

Finally, we decided to do the only thing two fifteen-year-olds could do at a time like this.

We decided to sneak into the back of the auditorium, quietly lodge ourselves on the back row, and slide down behind someone's head. Maybe, I thought, Mother wouldn't notice I wasn't on the second row, middle of the pew where I always sat. My mother not notice? What a joke! Maybe she would be distracted by my new baby sister, and for once, would NOT be "on the job."

Linda and I tiptoed over to the back row and sat down as the last stanza of the first hymn had been sung.

I could see the back of Mother's head as I tried to hide behind the lady in front of me, but I could see Mother winding up.

"Aahem," she began, as the frog settled firmly in her throat. Then she repeated it, exaggerating its loudness. As the second hymn was announced, the first verse began, and I saw the "turtle stretch" coming. It got higher and higher and her neck began to swivel in all directions, scanning the place for the sight of her number two daughter. I managed to dodge her search as I slid further down into the pew.

Mercifully, she swallowed the frog and she settled down. The neck returned to its rightful place on her shoulders, and I thought I was safe for the time being.

When brother McGaughey got up to preach, I poked Linda with my elbow and whispered. "Linda, I think we made it. Mother has quit looking around and she's just not sure I'm not up there, so I believe we can relax."

The next words I heard nearly knocked me off the pew! Brother McGaughey was standing quietly in front of the podium. He put his Bible down in front of him, got his glasses out of his coat pocket, put them on, and folded his hands piously over the Bible. In his most stoic, preacher-voice, he said:

"Brethren, I worked hard on my lesson for tonight, and I would really like to present it. I find it difficult to begin, however, because two of our lovely young ladies are on the back row and not up here where they belong. I will begin my sermon as soon as they have taken their places up here." And he waited. . . .

Instantly the "turtle stretch" preceded the frog. Mother was half out of her seat turning around. As every head in the congregation seemed pulled by a puppet string and turned toward us, we slowly got up and began the long walk to the front...

As I passed Mother, the "turtle-stretch" receded, but the frog got lodged once again and he was bigger and louder than ever!

When Linda and I finally got to the second row, about twenty-five kids had to re-shift two or three rows to make room for us. It was an eternity before we got situated. My face flushed and burned like it was on fire. I didn't look at Linda, and I sure didn't look at Mother!

It was the same for me at school as church. If I misbehaved, I got into trouble at home regardless of whose fault it was. I accused Mother of not loving me because she embarrassed me so much.

I was made to apologize to brother McGaughey and four years after the incident, when I was nineteen, he performed our wedding ceremony. Until his death, every time I saw him, he teased me about the "frog you caused in your mother's throat" that Sunday night so long ago!

MAGNET MESSAGE:

Give us an understanding of our youth, dear Father, helping us to realize that they want and need discipline and find security in knowing they are loved and cared about. In Jesus' Name, Amen.

"Remember now thy Creator in the days of thy youth, before the evil days draw nigh and you say, 'I have no pleasure in them.'" Ecclesiastes. 12:1

60. *The Classy Criterion*

The "waterfall" curtain slowly rises, the lights go down, and looking up, you see a simulated outdoor sky as thousands of "stars" begin to twinkle across the domed ceiling. The massive movie screen wraps itself around the stage and "sensor-sound" puts both action and sound all around you as the movie begins. Rows of majestic marble statues on their pedestals line the walls down the aisle on each side of the theater, and other statues stand stately in the lobby around the fountain.

The winding marble staircase that leads to the lounge is centered with a plush red carpet runner, and the brightly-lit lounge with its mirrored walls gives the area a look of infinity. The movie begins with a fanfare of music. Out front, the marquee blinks the movie title in bright, moving, neon lights.

You are at the Criterion Theater, Oklahoma City's finest and most elegant theater. A date to the Criterion means you are really special. The cost of a ticket is $1.00!

Your car is parked in front at a meter so you and your date can stroll Main Street afterwards or "drag Main" in your car in order to see who is going with the "new guy" or who broke up last night, or what's coming next to the Criterion. You will probably end up at Marlow's Drive-In (the 50's version of Sonic) to get the latest gossip.

In the early 1960's, the Criterion became a burlesque hall as the popularity of a new technology called TV jolted the movie industry almost out of existence. Enter urban renewal--and a dynamite blast collapsed the mighty Criterion into a heap of rubble. Ornate carvings, marble statues, and the glorious beauty of a rich heritage went up in smoke. When the dust settled, a new Oklahoma City, like a ghost, arose from the destruction.

Now in the midst of the "sexual revolution," a panicked Hollywood set out to regain the audience lost to TV. Movies began to increase in sleaze and the "X" rating was implemented. Never heard of before then, ratings became advertisements for the movie's immoral gutter language and perverted content. Theaters once again opened all over the city as they began to enjoy a resurgence of power and patronage.

A new generation, now desensitized, was ready to receive the "new movies" with their "new IMmorality" brought on by the winds of the social change of the 60's.

Gone are the sumptuous theater seats, the velvet curtains, the marble decor, the glittering ceiling, the magnificent movie musicals, movies that required no ratings, and gone is the era of elegance and grandeur in entertainment once offered by the Classy Criterion!

 MAGNET MESSAGE:

Give us, dear Lord, the wisdom to anticipate the approaching avalanche, and give us the courage to help halt it. In Jesus' name. Amen

"If my people, which are called by My name, shall humble themselves, and pray, and seek My face, and turn from their wicked ways; then will I hear from Heaven, and heal their land." II Chronicles 7:14

61. The Whuppin' Post

Exhausted, Mother sank into her chair. In the back bedroom, the loud giggles, squeals, and screams of two little girls grew louder. Mother was 45 years old, and having had her last child at age 40, she did not always have the energy that she had enjoyed with her first three children.

Daddy walked through the door just as the noise reached its highest peak, followed by the sound of bed slats and a headboard crashing to the floor!

Mother never allowed us to "burden your father with the problems of the day," and never threatened us with "Just wait until your daddy gets home!" She always said that Daddy had his hands full making a living, and he did not want to come through the door and hear about all the things that had gone wrong during a day. She insisted that our home be Daddy's "comfort zone," and if anything ever arose that she couldn't handle, then--and only then--would she burden him with it.

The night the bed fell apart must have been one of those times. The timing was off for her because it happened as Daddy came in, and, in her tired state, she was forced to turn the reins of discipline over to him, something she almost never did. She felt she should spare him all the worries she could. As the loud "explosion" in the back room erupted, Mother quietly said, "Morris, I guess you'll have to handle this one. I am simply too tired."

Meanwhile back on the bed, my two little sisters had been

using it as a trampoline--before there was such a thing--and it had totally collapsed. The mattress lay between the side rails, the headboard sprawled across it, and every slat was piled on the floor beneath the fallen mattress.

Daddy removed his belt and started down the hall. "Girls," he said loudly, "You're both getting a whuppin'!"

Opening the door, he whispered, "Now you two holler every time I swat the bed post." Then he slapped the belt against the post; first one, then the other of them, yelled their little faces off. Leaning down, he put the bed back together, straightened up, and walked out, closing the door.

Dead silence. A grateful mother relaxed and closed her eyes where she sat in her chair. Inside the bedroom, two little girls, five and eight years old, stifled giggles as they made up the bed, replaced the pillows, and came into the living room.

Not until they were grown did our sisters tell Mother what REALLY happened that evening. When they did, I remember a loving, understanding smile crossing Mother's pleasant face. She had known all along.

MAGNET MESSAGE:

Sometimes, dear Father, when we are weary and tired, bring to our lives a humorous memory that can refresh us like the rain after a drought. In Jesus' name. Amen.

"Foolishness is bound in the heart of a child, but the rod of correction shall drive it from him." Proverbs 22:15

62. Three-D Movies

When movies came out in three-dimension, I was one of the first teens to go see what it was all about. I had a date to the Criterion Theater to see The Phantom of Rue Morgue, and I could hardly wait.

As we entered the theater, we were handed a pair of cardboard glasses with one red and one green cellophane lens. We were told to put them on before the movie began.

Because the theater was so crowded, we had to sit about three rows from the front. As the movie began, we found ourselves completely captivated by the realism and the feeling of actually being "in" the movie. The scene that left me completely unraveled, however, was when the body fell out of the chimney! The music swelled to a climatic peak and "plop!" that body landed right square dab in the middle of my lap!

I must have jumped out of my seat about two feet and yelled at the top of my voice! Then I was terribly embarrassed. Although the entire audience had screamed, no one's scream was as loud as mine. Everybody laughed at me, including many classmates who were there that night.

As we left the theater, we were told to drop the cardboard glasses in a box by the exit. In the weeks to follow, my date continued to tease me unmercifully about my "outbreak" at the Criterion Theater! And it wasn't long until everybody at school was

joining in on the teasing, and I heard about it for a long time afterward.

Just as wide screens, and curved screens that put the movie all the way around us, disappeared, so did Three-D movies. I always wondered why. Maybe they cost too much to produce?

When an occasional chance to view a Three-D movie comes along today, and I hear kids excitedly talking about it and "those crazy glasses" they had to wear, I smile to myself and think of Edgar Allen Poe's Phantom of the Rue Morgue when I saw the marvels of three dimension for the first time.

MAGNET MESSAGE:

Thank you, God for all the blessings You give us through memories. With them, all of the good things of life need never be really gone. In Jesus' name, Amen.

"He that is merry of heart, has a continual feast." Proverbs 15:15

63. *Rothschild's--Store of the Stars!*

When downtown Oklahoma City was a bustling city full of shoppers and browsers, a beautiful store called Rothschild's sat on the corner of Main and Harvey. It was a store everybody called "exclusive," and when I went to town I passed by its windows in absolute teenage awe, almost afraid to even look! It was said that dresses there were one-of-a-kind and if you could afford one, you would never, ever see anyone else wearing one like it. It sold the kind of clothes a teen like me could only dream about.

When I turned sixteen, I got my social security number and headed downtown to apply for a job. I wanted to work after school and on holidays and summers. Somehow I got up the nerve necessary to apply for that job at Rothschild's, and by some miracle, I was hired !It was thrilling to a young girl to be able to purchase clothing at a twenty percent discount, even items on sale.

I learned that Rothschild's was billed as "The Store of the Stars!" Miss Oklahoma was always outfitted there. Her custom-made gowns were stunningly beautiful, and she modeled them, walking around throughout the store.

The most exciting day of my teen years, however, came at Christmastime the first year I worked there. I was hired to wrap gifts for the holiday season, and the store spared no expense to allow their customers the most beautifully wrapped gifts in Oklahoma City! We were told to make all bows with at least three yards of satin ribbon, and we were at liberty to create them and the packages they adorned as elaborate as our heart desired. It was just so much fun trying to see how different we could make each one.

As I was hard at work trying to keep up with all of the orders, a young man walked up with several boxes of gifts for me to wrap for his girlfriend. With the line long and so much to do, I did not look up as I took the boxes to wrap. As I checked the contents for price tags, the man said, "Please wrap them in paper the color of the contents."

When I cut off the paper and measured the ribbon, the man asked, "Where do you go to high school, young lady?""I go to Northeast," I replied, and it was then that I looked up! My eyes met the most beautiful blue eyes I had ever seen. "I went to Central myself," he explained. (The old Central High School building now houses SW Bell Telephone Co. in Oklahoma City.) My mouth dropped open and I could not speak. The handsome man with the thick black hair styled in the "Elvis pompadour" style of the times, was wearing a Rothschild's pure silk smoking jacket, and his thick, black lashes, like whisk brooms, framed those beautiful blues.

It was Dale Robertson! I am afraid the long line of customers had to wait while we all talked to him. He was at the height of his career at that time and one of Hollywood's most popular actors. He bought all of his clothing at Rothschild's. It was an exciting day for a 16-year-old's first day on the job!

When urban renewal advanced into Oklahoma City with its demolition team, it erased forever from our sight the skyline

with which we had grown up. John A. Brown, Peyton Marcus, Halliburton, Kerr's and Rothschild's all disappeared. Even though Rothschild's survived awhile in other locations, it too finally vanished and nothing came forth to replace Rothschild's--Store of the Stars!

MAGNET MESSAGE:

Physical change is all around us, dear God, but You and Your love and care for us NEVER change. Thank You for that. In Jesus' name. Amen.

"Jesus Christ, the same yesterday, today and forever..." John 11:6

64. Youthful Yearnings

Do you ever get behind a driver who is going too slowly and you are in a hurry? Your nerves on edge, you push the car faster and angrily pass him, only to see that it is someone you know? Do you recall the embarrassment of such a situation? It needs to happen only once.

That "once" for me was a situation in which I found myself with those same embarrassing feelings. I was 16 years old, and I will never forget it. It made a profound impression on my life, and I vowed at that time that I would never let it happen to me again.

I was working in downtown Oklahoma City for Roths-child's Department Store, and I rode the bus to work every day when I got out of school, working until the store closed .My best friend rode too, and she worked for John A. Brown Department Store, across the street from Rothschild's.

Every single day, at the same bus stop, a lady got on; Mary Jo and I thought she was ancient. She was probably in her early forties. But that would have been "old" to us. We could hardly wait for the bus to pick her up because she provided us our laughs for the day. I can still see her in my mind! She had jet-black hair that she pulled up into little braids on top of her head. Tiny, bouncy, cork-screw curls, like little springs, dangled all around her face, and her lashes, heavy with mascara, looked like black widow spiders!

Mary Jo and I stifled the giggles as best we could, but her manner of dress was even more hysterical than her face. She wore yards and yards of ruffles and lace, and she cinched up her waist over her full skirts with glittering belts and hanging beads. Her shoes were either gold or silver, and on top of her head amidst the braids and curls were combs interwoven with all kinds of flowers, and she wore the brightest, reddest lipstick we had ever seen.

We thought she was the funniest looking woman in the world, and we couldn't wait for her to get on the bus everyday to see what she was wearing. We laughed all the way to work and nicknamed her "Miss Priss."

During our teen years growing up in Oklahoma City, we children spent a great part of our lives going to church. In those days, a Gospel Meeting, or Revival, would usually last about two weeks.

Our entire family always attended all of the area-wide meetings of that time, so our visits often took us to neighboring churches where we saw many old friends, and met new ones, too. During one such Gospel Meeting, we arrived early as usual and took our seat near the front. As I sat there, I noticed a woman come in the back door and walk down to the front to sit.

I slid down the seat as I realized it was "Miss Priss!" I was shocked! I was also afraid she would see me. My fears were soon realized. She did! She smiled sweetly as she walked on by, and I thought maybe she hadn't realized that I was the smart alec teenager who rode her bus everyday.

I had never told Mother about the "funny woman" on the bus, so she did not understand my anxious need to leave so quickly after services. She and Daddy were used to me staying around TOO long and having to wait on me because there were always new faces of the opposite sex for me to meet.

During the time I was begging Mother to "come on--let's go," Miss Priss walked up.

"May I speak with you, Honey," she asked sweetly. I died. But I told her she certainly could.

"I know that you and your girlfriend laugh at me every day when I get on your bus." I felt my face burning. Here was a lovely woman, obviously my sister in Christ, and I had hurt her. She continued:

"My husband just died recently and his last words to me were, 'Sweetheart, stay young, don't ever dress or act old, or you will be, and don't ever let anyone put you down or make you feel silly for wanting to stay young and look young.' And so, my dear, that is exactly what I do and will continue to do as long as I live. I am sorry if you find that funny."

I hung my head in shame. I promised myself never to let anything like that happen again. To this day, I think of her when I get impatient with people I do not know--like in traffic, an elevator, or in the line at the grocery store, or any other situation that puts me on the defense. I have one quick thought of Miss Priss and the lesson she gave me that night. And the ironic thing about it all, I am just like her; I love yards of lace, ribbons and ruffles--wonder how many have laughed at me? (Seems like I recall we "reap what we sow.")I never saw Miss Priss again and I wonder. . . was she "an angel unaware" to teach me that night so long ago, this unforgettable lesson?

MAGNET MESSAGE:

Give us patience to deal with life's trials, and let us learn from our mistakes as we strive to be more like YOU. In Jesus' name, Amen.

"…some have entertained angels unaware…" Hebrews 13:2

65. *Baseball is the Name of the Game*

Beautiful moonlit summer nights with all of the stars out were special to us growing up. Mother popped a huge bowl of corn, filled glasses with iced lemonade, and we would pile outside on a blanket in the back yard and look up at the sky. We would locate the Big Dipper; munch on popcorn, and discus any and everything.

Daddy put the radio in the window, turned up the volume, and we listened to the Oklahoma City Indians play baseball at Texas League Park. We guessed what the final score would be and spent the evening rooting for the players we knew by their first names. Some evenings we went to the games, but sometimes we just stayed home and listened to the radio.

By the time I was a teenager, the game was really a part of my life, and I had grown to love it. One time when I was a student council officer from my high school, my picture appeared on the "Teen Page" of the Oklahoma City Times, the evening paper back then. Every week, the Times printed news from all of Oklahoma City's high schools on a page they called "The Times for Teens."

A few days after the picture appeared, I received a letter from a young man from Lawton who had seen the picture and decided to write to me. He was stationed at Ft. Sill and was a baseball player. He told me he aspired to someday be a great pitcher and had played in the Oklahoma Farm System. He had plans to make it a career as soon as he finished his hitch in the army.

His letter told me he had been drafted into the army and was putting his ball-playing career on hold pending such time as he was discharged from the army. I was interested in pursuing this correspondence since I loved baseball. We wrote for awhile and we exchanged photos. I had not realized how many years my senior he was, and when I did find out, I decided to discourage the developing friendship. I was only sixteen. He wrote me that he had bought a new car and was anxious to drive up in it to see me. Because of the age difference, I got cold feet and soon afterward, he was shipped overseas. At that point, I discontinued the communication, and soon forgot about him.

Years later, I was watching the World Series, and a handsome pitcher took the mound. The TV camera zoomed in on the young man's face, and as he took off his hat, the breeze caught a wisp of his beautiful blond hair and blew it across his forehead. As he wiped his brow and replaced his hat, I heard the man over the sound system announce his name. Instantly, I recalled the last letter I had received from the young man stationed at Ft. Sill. It read: ". . . .and my hair is so blond that folks call me 'Whitey,'--Whitey Ford!"

MAGNET MESSAGE:

Help us to realize that You guide our lives in accordance with Your will, if we will let You. In Jesus' name, Amen.

"The Lord knows the thoughts of men...." Psalm 94:11

66. The Old Trunk

It was an old, weatherworn trunk, and I remember well the first time I saw it. It was filled to the brim with all sorts of accessories such as jewelry, hats, and shoes that my grandmother had worn. When I visited her as a young child, she let me open it and play with everything in it if I wanted to.

Years later, I was to learn that the old trunk had bumped and bounced around in a covered wagon while traveling across Oklahoma during the days when Oklahoma was Indian Territory.

I thought the hats were especially beautiful, but looking back at them in my memory, I realize they would have looked extremely funny by today's standards. There were net veils covered with velvet polka dots attached to little satin pill-box types, and big, bulky brims covered with bird feathers, and some of them were even decorated with plastic fruit such as bananas, pears, and grapes.

There was one item of beauty tucked into the velvet-pleated pouch on the inside of the lid that especially caught my fancy. It was my grandmother's graduation dress. It must have been magnificent in its hey-day. It was soft net layered into three tiers, and covered with embroidered flowers. The puffed sleeves were attached to a pink satin-lined lace yoke, and the high collar was a ruffle of solid lace. The bodice and skirt were joined together with a big satin bow that had once been cotton-candy pink. I felt like a princess as I dragged around its hem and sagging sash behind me, as around and around I twirled.

I loved to put on that dress, top it with a hat covered with grapes, and prance around my grandmother's house--and even outside. I put on her glasses and strands of her beads and then added her "ear bobs." The crystal ones dangled from my ears like clear drops of iridescent colors.

When I entered my senior year of high school, I was part of a group of drama students who were taking our one-act play, The Six Wives of Henry VIII, to the state speech tournament. I was to play the part of Ann Seymour, and the story line consisted of all eight of Henry's wives arising from the grave to meet him in a banquet hall and learn which of his six wives he had really loved. To look as if I had been in the grave for some time, my drama teacher instructed me to find a dress to wear that would best fit that situation. The memory of the fading lace dress instantly came to my mind.

The trunk had taken up residence in our attic after my grandmother's death, and until now, had almost been forgotten. The rusty hinges squeaked as I lifted the wobbly lid, but there in its pouch underneath it, where it had been for many years, lay the dress, its lace no longer white, but aged as if someone had poured diluted tea on it.

I carefully lifted it out, noticing how easily it could tear, and anxiously, but very carefully, I tried it on. It was a perfect fit. As a little girl, I had often dreamed of the dress fitting me someday.

My drama teacher was pleased with my selection, and even more so when she learned the story behind it. We presented our one-act play at the tournament, and in the ghostly smoke that the prop crew created onstage, I floated out in a gown that a young woman had worn on her graduation day over half a century earlier. I am sure I felt her presence.

And the tournament? Well...our group took first....

MAGNET MESSAGE:

You are our Guiding Light, Dear Lord, no matter where we go. We may be filled with questions, but we know that You ever care for Your own. Thank You for standing by us. In Jesus' name, Amen.

"Lord, I put my hope in you; I have trusted in you since I was young." Psalm 71:5

67. Those Pretty Green Leaves

I looked down at the engagement ring just placed on my finger. I sure did wish that I could see it. My fiancé had chosen it for me and I thought how nice it would be if I could just look at it!

Looking through slits where my eyes should have been, I thought I saw a twinkle, but I was miserable the night that should have been my happiest.

My entire face--especially my eyes--was swollen and puffy, coated heavily with the calamine lotion I was wearing for make-up. What a sight I was! I wondered if my dark tan had been worth it.

I thought back to that morning when a friend and I had decided to go spend a relaxing day at the lake. We found a secluded spot at a privately-owned lake where we could soak up some rays, swim, and picnic before we had to go to work. We worked the late shift at Southwestern Bell Telephone Company as operators to help pay our college expenses, and did not have to report to work until 10:00 pm.

After swimming for awhile, we decided to sunbathe, and I realized that I forgot my sunglasses. "It's okay," my friend, Freida said. "I read in a magazine that dipping leaves in the water and placing them on your eyes protects them as well as sunglasses."

That sounded good to me, and as I spread my beach towel and settled myself under the hot summer sunshine, I noticed a little vine creeping across the ledge above my head. I reached up and pulled a couple of leaves, dipped them in the lake water, and placed them on my closed eyelids. As I was enjoying the warmth of the day, I thought what a good idea this had been. My eyes felt cool and comfortable. Better than sunglasses, I thought.

When I got home, my eyes began to itch...and itch... By the time my husband-to-be arrived with the "surprise" he had for me, my eyes were too swollen to see anything but narrow slivers of light.

He had the ring in his pocket and when he saw me, I wondered if he would change his mind! Since my hands were also swelling, it was difficult to get it on my finger! This was not funny!

I eventually had to go to the doctor who said I was lucky that I did not lose my eyesight. "Weren't you a Girl Scout, or something?" he asked. "Don't you know poison ivy when you see it?"

 MAGNET MESSAGE:

Thank you, Father, for your gentle care and love. Thank you for overlooking the vanities of youth and guiding us into the things that are important in this life as we mature in Christ Jesus. In Jesus' name, Amen.

"So now, Christ shall be magnified in my body, whether it be by life, or by death." Philippians 1:20

68. "Just give me what you think she's worth!"

While cleaning out what I thought was an old box of junk, I came across a 5x7 green box with "Gene Cotton, Photographer, Oklahoma City, Oklahoma" stamped on the outside. I opened it, and inside, the soiled white cover of a book glared up at me.

"The wedding of Freddy and Molly" was stamped in gold on the worn binding, and I realized just how long it had been since the photos inside had been taken.

My thoughts went back to January 25, 1957, when I had become the bride of Freddy Lemmons. "Just give me what you think she's worth," Brother C.E. McGaughey told Freddy after the ceremony when asked about his fee.

A handsome rascal and an outstanding athlete, Freddy had caught my fancy when I first met him on the campus of Oklahoma Christian when I was a freshman there.

The night we married, almost 43 years ago, it was snowing and the snow was freezing as fast as it was hitting the ground. But inside the church of Christ at 36th and Prospect in Oklahoma City, it was warm and beautiful. My four attendants, each in a different shade of blue, glided down the aisle carrying pink fans adorned with feathered pink carnations, streamers, and blue ribbons.

Since blue is my favorite color, it was everywhere. Blue pew bows, blue candles, blue flowers, and even the light bulbs on the ceiling of the auditorium had been replaced with blue bulbs.

The wedding was a family affair. My older sister, Sally, was my Maid of Honor; my brother, Bob, at age 15 was an usher. My little sister, Polly Pat was a candle lighter, and Baby Ellen, 5, was flower girl.

A group sang "Thee I Love," "Friendly Persuasion" (a Pat Boone favorite of the times), "True Love" (a Bing Crosby-Grace Kelly duet), the ever-beautiful hymns, "My God and I," "Tell Me Why," and of course, the "Wedding March."

I do not feel any different today than I did 43 years ago until I am reminded of the fact that more years now lie behind us than lie ahead of us, and this is a sobering reminder.

Forty-three years! Where have they gone? In my heart, I feel it was only yesterday that I stepped out into that aisle and floated, in my wide hoop and "Scarlet O'Hara" wedding dress, to join my life and heart to the one I had chosen to be my mate "until death parts us."

There have been sorrows: the loss of loving parents, and bouts of ill health, but numerous blessings have sprinkled our lives with their sweetness--the best of these having been our children! Given to us through adoption by the loving providence of God, we often prayed to be worthy of the honor to be their parents.

Without tears in marriage--and there have been many--smiles cannot be appreciated. He used to say, "I wish we could bottle your tears and sell them--we would be so rich!" Tears? Yes. Smiles? Yes, there have been many.

When I think of him, I think of the funny way he crinkles

up his nose and sniffs when he is caught not knowing what to say. I think of the pictures of myself I put between his sandwiches when I sent him off to work. I think of the love notes I tucked into his pockets, and the whispered phone calls to him on the job.

I think of all the silly tricks he pulled on me. Like telling me on the phone that he was going to "blow out the lines and to cover the mouth piece on the phone so the dust won't cover the kitchen cabinets."

I think of the smiles of our children and the joy they bring. The cute things they said that often brought us to our knees in laughter and thanksgiving.

Yes, 43 years since the preacher said, "Just give me what you think she's worth."

He has never told me the amount he gave brother McGaughey, but I have reason to believe it was a whopping TEN DOLLARS!

"What God has joined together, let not man put asunder." Mark 10:9

69. "I Knew I Should Have Measured You Myself"

We sat in the hospital waiting room watching for the doctor to come in with the report of the one in surgery. When he emerged from surgery after only 15 minutes, we knew the news was not good. To my husband and his siblings, the doctor stated firmly and to the point: "Your mother has about three weeks to live at the most. The cancer is the worse kind. I just sewed her back up."

Tears blurred my eyes, and I became lost in thought as his voice droned on and on...I did not hear what he was saying. I was caught up in the flashback memories of the 36 years she been my mother-in-law.

Mother-in-law jokes are as old as history itself. Even if you love your mother-in-law, it's never been in vogue to say so. Mothers-in-law are supposed to be the epitome of bossiness, and to be forever interfering in your lives. I have been made to feel uncomfortable because I did not regard my mother-in-law in this manner.

She was a black-eyed beauty. Her eyes sparkled with mischief every time she flashed her lovely smile. Her snow-white teeth were straight and beautiful, and she took great pride in taking care of herself. She was the grandmother of eight and great-grandmother of ten, but while she was not your ordinary

"Granny" or "Grandma," she did not project the image of a "Toots," a "Bambi," or "Kitty," as some of today's career-minded, younger-than-ever grandmothers do. Hers was a marvelous mixture somewhere in between, the best of both worlds.

Her sense of humor was constant. If she missed a day without a trick or a joke, you knew she wasn't feeling well. She teased and played constantly, and her laughter and giggles continually filled the house.

She was an accomplished seamstress, and she thrived on making beautiful garments for the entire family. She shopped for fabric bargains, and her little "textile trunk" was running over with all sorts of fabrics just waiting for the right pattern.

Through the years, she made many dresses, blouses, and skirts for me, most of them one-of-a-kind or a copy of one I had seen in a store window. I had only to ask. Once I requested a white wool pleated skirt, and she asked me what my waist measured. I replied, "Twenty-two inches." (I knew full well I had not been 22 inches since high school, but I was on a diet, and after all, I would be down to that by the time she got the skirt made.)

She worked long and hard on that skirt, measuring each little pleat 1/2 inch in width, and she steam pressed it into place. The white pleated skirt was beautiful! Just one thing was wrong: The waistband lacked a good three inches coming together when I tried to button it. She shook her long, slender finger at me and said, "I knew I should have measured you myself." She took out all the pleats, ripped out the seams, steam pressed the wool, and started all over. Through the years, the while wool pleated skirt became a sort of legend, but it always evoked the same response from her: "I knew I should have measured you myself!"

I was sitting there in the hospital thinking how good it was that we had never exchanged any cross words, especially since I know there must have been times she wanted to work me over. Like the time I cheated a little-just three inches--on what my waist had measured. She had every right to be upset, but the incident became a family joke that endured for 30 years.

"...so surround her with family and love for the time she has left," I heard the doctor saying as my spinning head pivoted my thoughts back to the hospital room.

My dear mother-in-law lived one year and 11 days from that day, her sparkling personality and snappy black eyes never fading until that last day. Then she quietly said, "I am going to die today." And she did.

MAGNET MESSAGE:

Give us, Dear Heavenly Father, moments with our families to treasure as time passes by so swiftly. Thank you for the happy memories of a dear mother-in law. In Jesus' name, Amen.

"...and Orpah kissed her mother-in-law but Ruth held on to her." Ruth 1:14

70. The Hair Dye Dilemma

For as long as I can remember, Mother has had gray hair. Not always as much as now, but the graying process came so early in her life, that to me, it just seemed to have always been like that.

As a child, the gray hair bothered me--a lot! I thought it meant she was going to die soon, and as the hair got whiter and whiter, I worried more about it.

When I went with her to the grocery store, I would sneak over to the hair care products and slip a box of hair dye in her grocery cart. When we got to the checkout stand, I would divert her attention with some silly comment as the checker came to the conspicuous little package. I never got away with it.

"Molly Lou Rogers," she would say, "You march yourself right back over there and put this back on the shelf!" I always knew it was serious business when she used my entire name. I did this every time I went with her to the store, and every time I had to put it back.

Mother grew up in an era when "a lady did not tint her hair." Sort of like the era in which I grew up--"a lady did not pierce her ears." Boys at school always whispered about "those girls with the pierced ears." Mother could not shake the image of those women in her day who colored their hair any more than I--years later--could shake the image of the girls in my generation who pierced their ears.

It would take years to adjust to the cultural shock--and most of us do adjust, but some of us never do--and Mother was one who never did.

There was one time, however, that almost caused Mother to change her mind. She was almost forty years old when she gave birth to Baby Ellen, the youngest of the five of us. By then her hair was silver white on top and around her face. When Ellen was in kindergarten, Mother went to pick her up one day, and a friend was sitting with Ellen on the school steps. When Mother drove up, she saw the little girl lean over and say something to Ellen. Of course, Mother couldn't hear what she said, but Ellen raised her arm and gave the girl a hard smack across the face. The, with tears, she ran to the car.

She threw her arms around Mother's neck and hugged her. "What was that all about?" Mother asked.

Sobbing, Ellen spluttered, as she told Mother that the girl had said, "Better go, there's your grandmother!" For one fleeting moment, Mother was tempted to cover her gray--but she never gave in to that temptation; the upbringing of her day was imprinted just too vividly in her memory.

When I turned thirty, it just seemed the thing to do to color my hair. I knew the toll it would take on Mother and how her impression of me could be jeopardized, but I decided to do it anyway. Thirty just seemed so old, and besides, dyed hair no longer held the connotation that it had in Mother's day.

Mother always made a big deal over our birthdays, no matter which one it was, and being thirty was no exception. When she got the cake and gifts and had me come over to celebrate, I appeared at the door with my jet-black "do". She would not let

me in. I thought she was going to cry.

"I don't want to look at you like that," she said. "The Lord blessed you with beautiful hair and you have ruined it." And she closed the door. She was exactly right. It proved to be the worst thing I had ever done. My hair was very long and the bottom five inches turned a brassy red. I had to cut it off. Then the next five inches turned brassy red. I had to cut it off. Then the next five inches, and so on. I ended up with a shaved neckline hair cut to get it all off.

When I look at Mother today with her shiny, snowy, silvery hair, I am thankful she was always strong in her convictions and just to satisfy my childish notion that "white hair means impending death," never gave in to the "hair dye dilemma."

MAGNET MESSAGE:

Help us to do our best, but we know that even though we sometimes fail, You will accept us, loving us unconditionally. In Jesus' Name, Amen.

"Do not thou, O lord, withhold thy mercy from me, let thy steadfast love and thy faithfulness ever preserve me!" Psalm 40:11

71. *"I understand exactly how you feel!"*

As a young wife, I sat at the desk across from the doctor, and heard him say as gently and as firmly as he could, "My dear, you will never give birth, but I can assure you that I understand."

Understand? I wanted to scream! How could you, Mr. Doctor, possibly understand? I began to sob incessantly and automatically reached for the box of Kleenex that he was holding out to me.

I heard his voice drone on and on. "There, there, it isn't all that bad," he kept repeating, and never in my life had I had such an urge to slap anyone. The nerve of him, thinking that it was "all right," "not so bad," and that he understood! I wanted to shout at him and ask him if he knew what it was like to hear my young friends talk of their babies, to go to baby showers, and to pass the racks of baby clothes at the store.

He couldn't even begin to comprehend, I thought, what it was like to be told that the dream I had of being a mother--the only thing I ever really desired--was gone forever. Did he know what it was like to live next door to a sixteen-year-old girl and see her go through three abortions? Did he know what it was like to watch this girl continually trash human life while my arms were aching to hold what she was throwing away?

Until he had felt all of these emotions and seen these injustices, no, he most certainly did not understand! I just kept asking him over and over, "Is it really true?" Not waiting for his answers, I continued with the questions and the pleading. "Maybe it was a mistake, maybe the test was not accurate...could we run another one?"

The doctor assured me that the test had been correct and added, "Don't worry, there are other alternatives, and I understand exactly how you feel!" What a hypocrite, I thought, he can sit here in his thousand-dollar suit behind his massive solid oak desk with his big, fat payroll and tell ME that he understands? I didn't believe him for one minute. In fact, I felt if he said much more, I would smack him right square across the mouth!

Hatred--pure and simple--for this doctor surged into my heart. I was so angry that I did not see him rise from his chair and stand, turning his back to me, as I sat sobbing, my head on his desk.

When I looked up, I thought he must surely be the most egotistical, smart-alec doctor in the whole world, and he had just proven it by turning his back on me.

Sensing the intense emotion of the situation and without retaliation against my heart-broken anger, the doctor quietly went about removing some photographs from his cabinet and placing them on the desk in front of me.

"Do you see the two children in these pictures?" he asked kindly. I wiped my tears, and as the blurred photos of the babies came into focus, my body and spirit, by now emotionally depleted, began to relax.

"My wife and I were also unable to have children," the doctor continued, as I slowly brought my attention around to what he was saying.

"These two precious babies were chosen through the avenue of adoption. There really are other options, and yes, my dear, I DO understand exactly how you feel."

MAGNET MESSAGE:

For those of us, Dear Father, who hope and pray for babies, we give thanks to those unselfish women who choose adoption for their children rather than abortion; for without them, many of us would never know the joy a baby can bring into a home. In Jesus' name, Amen.

"The fear of the Lord is the beginning of wisdom..." Proverbs 9:10

72. What Could Be Sweeter Than This?

I want to be a mother when I grow up!"

It was with a proud arrogance that I spoke these words at age eleven when my baby sister was born. I got to help take care of her and I was convinced that was exactly what I wanted to "do" with my life when I grew up! My memories of taking care of a real, live doll grew in my mind to be so wonderful that I couldn't wait to get married and have at least five children!

But alas! After eight years of marriage my dream was still not realized. With each passing month, my longing intensified and my sorrow magnified. There seemed to be no answers, and even my prayers seemed to be ignored. Through the kind remarks of a caring physician who had adopted his children, we began to think of other ways to be a parent.

So it finally happened: On the 10th of November 1964, a drizzly rain fell outside, and I was home from work feeling sick. Another month and another disappointment, and I just went to bed, rolled up in a blanket, and told my husband not to call me to the phone or the door; I wanted to see no one. I had almost reached my limit for the disappointments that had besieged me during these disappointing years.

From my bedroom, I heard the faint ring of the living room phone. I pulled the cover higher over my head and buried myself deeper into my pillow. My husband eased open my door and whispered:

"Molly Lou, get up and get dressed. We need to go down and pick up our baby girl!"

Within thirty minutes, we were sitting in a room awaiting the "delivery" of our little girl. The rain outside could no longer squelch the sunshine that had begun to glow within my heart. Shortly, a small bundle was placed in my arms.

I turned back the pink blanket to reveal its contents. Peering back at me were two of the biggest, brightest, eyes I had ever seen! Those enormous, dazzling eyes were framed with porcelain white creamy skin, while a tuft of golden auburn hair surrounded her little head like a tiny copper halo.

I again whispered the prayer that I had sent up to God so often. I had been telling Him for eight long years, that if He ever saw fit to give me a baby, that I would, like Hannah of the Bible, return her to Him by "training her up in the way she should go."

"A baby, my very own baby…" I kept repeating as I gazed into her tiny face. I could not believe that any human being could feel what I was feeling. As the blanket fell away, also falling away with it were the painful memories that brought me—finally, to this beautiful moment. The memory of the many long years of fertility tests, disappointments, failures, and trips to the doctor now dissolved into oblivion as I looked upon this baby—the greatest gift God ever gave me! Every emotion known to mankind overwhelmed my very being and my tears splashed on her small face; emotions of joy, respect, compassion, thanksgiving, love and gentleness. The sorrow and sadness of the previous years were completely erased.

All the years I had longed for, and prayed for, had finally

culminated in this, a precious baby girl selected just for me! When her petite face first appeared from beneath the blanket, I noticed the corners of her little rose bud mouth turned up into a sweet smile—and I thought, surely we had adopted an angel.I lifted her out of her blanket-cocoon and cuddled her to my breast. We named her Lucinda because it means light, and she was certainly that! What could possibly be sweeter than this? I was besieged with God's Goodness and my heart was so full, it felt as if it would literally burst inside my chest.

We took her home and she became the delight of our lives, amazing us with her calm disposition, intelligence, and happy demeanor. She giggled, sang, and danced her way into all our hearts, and became the darling of our family. She knew, without a doubt, that she was loved, wanted, and treasured, and she returned to me all of the happiness and joy I felt I had lost during the preceding years when I yearned for a baby.

True to my promise to God, I taught her Scriptures daily and by the age of two-and-a-half, she could name all sixty-six books of the Bible. She could name the four Gospels, and the five books of Law; her favorite story was Daniel in the Lion's Den. By the time she was grown, she was well versed in those Scriptures from the Books she had learned when so young. She amazed everyone with her intellect and wisdom, not just in spiritual matters, but in secular matters as well.

Adopting her sent me blessings I knew not existed. God often answers our prayers in ways we do not expect.

What could be sweeter than this?

MAGNET MESSAGE:

Not a day goes by that I am not thankful for my two "adopted angels" that God sent me after years of doubt and questions. Thank you, God, for these blessings. In Jesus' name, Amen.

"O Lord Almighty, if you will only remember me, and not forget your servant but give her a son, then I will give him to the Lord for all the days of his life..." I Samuel 1:11

3. Unheard Utterings

Hey! Precious little girl--you look so vulnerable asleep there in your bed with that beautiful auburn hair swirling in curls around your face. I'd love to brush those little ringlets of damp curls from your face, but it might wake you. I can't seem to get much done during the time since we got you. Time is passing so swiftly, and it will be only a short time before you begin school. I do not want to waste a moment of the time allotted to me for enjoying you. There is so much I want to tell you and teach you that I worry I won't have enough time to get it all into that little computer-like brain of yours.

You are the greatest gift I could receive! I prayed for you so long, I began to worry that I wasn't being heard. Boy, was I wrong! God was saving something special for me. That is one of the beauties of adoption--God decides the time and circumstances, and in the process, teaches patience.

Since you left your crib for this "big bed," you seem small all over again. I want to cuddle you in my arms, rock you, and protect you from the world. I want to shield your innocent mind and gentle heart, and keep you close and safe all of your life. But this is not to be. You must grow and I must let you go. That is the hardest part of all. Will I have taught you what you need to know to sustain you through life? Will I have taught you to care for your spiritual being as well as your physical? Will you understand how life can be death and death can be life? That the separation from this life is temporary, but the reunion in the next life is eternal? Will I have equipped you to handle all of these things?

I wish you had come with up-bringing instructions stamped on your little neck, like washing instructions come stamped on a shirt, because by the time I realize all of my mistakes, it will be too late.

I keep thinking of the first time I saw you. I opened up that little blanket and those enormous eyes as big as quarters on that tiny face shone like clear, liquid pools against that china porcelain skin.

We continually marvel at your intelligence. When Charles Holleyman was over here last night, he gave you a little test. Charles is Mustang's Superintendent of Schools, and he just loves to test children he thinks are "extra smart" as he puts it. When you finished the test, he said, "Well, there's Mustang's 1982 Valedictorian"* and you know? I believe him, too. You can reason out almost any situation and are such a wise little pre-schooler. You have so blessed my life that I spend a greater part of my day in thanksgiving.

I've been here beside your bed about an hour now, thinking of this awesome responsibility I have been given. I feel you are a loan to us, and we are obligated to give you back to God.

I wish I could tell you it would be easy. I wish I could tell you life will be fair; I can't, but I can tell you God will be fair. I wish I could tell you that you will never hurt and never cry, but I cannot. I can tell you that Jesus hurt, and He wept, too.

I can tell you that for every temptation, there is a way out. For every hurt, there is a comforting scripture and God is only a

prayer away. For every rainstorm, there will be a rainbow, and every thorn, a rose. The choices will be yours, and I pray they will be choices based on Scripture and what you know to be right.

Now I will kiss this sweet little cheek goodnight and tell you, our precious little daughter, just how very much you were wanted and how very much you are loved. No matter what the future brings, you will always be our "Adopted Angel," and don't you ever forget it. Since I know that you cannot hear any of these utterings, I will write them down so that someday you may read the things that were on my heart this night as you slept.

Footnote: I wrote this beside Lucinda's bed as she slept. She was two years old .It was November 1966. Just three months later, we got our precious baby boy, Roger.

*Lucinda was Valedictorian of Mustang Schools in 1982

74. Not of my Flesh

When Lucinda was six months old, we had to go to court to legally adopt her. The six-month waiting period was a "trial period" to see if the baby would be compatible with our lifestyle and us. (Silly? I think so--what birth mother ever sends her baby "back?")

As we sat before Judge Homer Smith, he asked us, "Do you want to adopt this baby?" Again, rage filled my heart! What a stupid, stupid question, I thought! I just burst into tears. A kind and gentle man, Judge Smith explained that he was "supposed to ask that." He could see exactly what I was thinking, and he was supportive and caring. We left there after signing the final papers and re-opening our application with the possibility of a baby boy for later. Then we left to visit friends and to show off our new baby girl. Happiness that only a baby can bring had come to our home at last!

The man directly responsible for placing Lucinda in our arms had died of cancer. Before he died, he told me that he wouldn't be around to get us a boy, but for me to call every day and pester them until I got some action. With Lucinda almost two, it was time to start pestering.

At that time, thirty-five was the age limit for an infant and I was approaching thirty. I felt there was no time to wait. I called every day and sometimes two or three times a day.

Finally, when Lucinda was two-and-a-half, the call came. It was February 23, 1967, and we were to come pick up our baby boy. The day was overcast in gloomy clouds and a chilling wind blew from the north, but the warmth in my heart concealed every negative thing about the day. To me, the sun was bright and the air was warm. My maiden name was Rogers and my mother's name was Pauline so our little boy with the thick black hair, long lashes and blue, blue eyes became "Roger Paul."

When he was six months old, we again stood before Judge Homer Smith. He remembered us from the time before, and this time, only said, "There is no doubt you want this baby!" We signed the papers and again stopped to show off our new baby boy. The following Sunday morning, we were surrounded with good wishes as we crossed the church parking lot. Little Lucinda was lost in the shuffle and for the first time in her short life, she did not want to go to Bible class.

Some kind words from an older member of the church encouraged me to keep her beside me and let her hold her new baby brother. I was forever thankful for the wisdom of that older woman.

As with Lucinda's adoption, we re-opened our application for other children following our adoption of Roger, but as I approached age thirty-five, and the waiting lists were growing longer and longer, our chances became slimmer and slimmer that it would ever happen again. I continued to call and pester and was finally told not to be selfish, that I had two; others waiting had none. So with the sadness that the finality of it all brought, I withdrew to accept the fact that I would never again know the joy that my very own baby would bring into my life.

I was grateful for the two I had, and never ceased to let God know that I was thankful for them and sorry for my impatience and near hostility towards Him during those trying years in which I almost lost my faith as I again and again failed to conceive. As the legalization of abortion became law, I found myself becoming bitter and angry that women could throw away babies like the morning garbage, while my arms ached to hold what they were tossing away. But now, finally, I had realized a dream come true, and I held my second baby in my arms with thanksgiving.

With the final papers signed and Roger legally ours, the summer season of my heart was beginning to turn warm, beautiful and wonderful after all!

"Not of my own flesh
But just as much mine.
Not taken by chance
But chosen for all time!
Carried for nine months
In the body of another,
I will carry you forever,
I am your mother!"

MAGNET MESSAGE:

No one will ever know the full extent of the joy I received upon Your giving us our babies. In a world where they are thrown away daily, I consider them a special gift for my everlasting love and care. Thank you so much for allowing me to be blessed in such a very special way. I pray the world will come back to You and once again realize that children are the best of all the gifts You give us. In Jesus' Name, Amen

"Children's children are the crown of old men and the glory of children are their fathers." Proverbs 17:5

75. The Cedar Chest

The refreshing, clean, unmistakable odor of cedar filled my nostrils as I opened my cedar chest sitting silently in its place at the foot of the bed. Covered with a tapestry and pillows, it was often forgotten until the need arose to open it to retrieve some memento from the past.

When I graduated from high school, I took all of the money that I had received in gifts and bought the limed oak Lane cedar chest in which, during the years to come, I would store all of my precious memories.

My senses filled with the sweet images of the past as I raised the lid, and the sweet aroma filled the air.

First, I removed my wedding dress in order to get to the bottom of the chest for a copy of my high school diploma. The dress was as bright and white as the night I wore it except for the gray edges around the hem, which stood as testimony of that snowy night so long ago.

There were many things in the chest, but the ones that most caught my eye and my sentiment were not so much the wedding dress and veil, or even the wedding book, but it was the two small bundles wrapped neatly and placed in the corner on the bottom of the chest.

It had been some time since I had opened the chest, so I

picked up the two little bundles. The first one was a yellow flannel blanket, and inside was a tiny white gown and matching slip lightly embroidered with dainty roses around the hem and neckline. Two small shoes with bells in the laces rolled out as I picked it up.

The other blanket was flannel also with crocheted edging. Inside was a little shirt with a baseball and bat embroidered on the pocket, and a pair of tiny britches to match. White leather shoes rolled out of that blanket as I picked it up.

I was immediately taken back to when we adopted our babies. I'll never forget a dreary, rainy day in November 1964 that turned out to be the brightest day in all my life as I held our baby daughter in my arms for the very first time.

I will always remember a cold, blustery, cloudy day in February 1967 when I first held our baby boy, and wondered how I could be more blessed than I was at that very moment.

I spread the baby clothes out on the bed and ran my fingers over each piece as I was taken back to a time when the sweet, warm babies wore them, and could smell the Baby Magic lotion, the Johnson's Baby Powder, and yes, even the Nestles Baby Curl. Where had the years gone? How had they gone so quickly?

My arms ached to hold, just one more time, those little darlings in my arms; to brush the moist curls from their faces; to kiss the chubby cheeks, and hug away their heartaches. It would even be welcome to bandage a skinned knee again, to hold them close and protect them from the world outside and make them secure in knowing how very much they are loved.

MAGNET MESSAGE:

Thank you, God for giving us our two precious children. Forgive me when I became impatient with Your timetable and insisted on mine. By waiting, You taught us not only patience, but also that really good things do come to those who wait. In Jesus' name, Amen.

"Before I formed you in the womb, I knew you..." Jeremiah 1:45

76. *"Don't Cry, Mommy"*

I 'm sure that there are parents out there who love their children as much as I love mine, but I am positive there are none out there who love them more! My dream to become a mother had come true through the adoption process, and although I had hoped to birth my children, I found there was no difference in the way I felt, and motherhood was all I had expected it to be. A mother is so much more than just one who gives birth; the meaning of the word, mother, entails a volume of feelings; dedication, love, unselfishness, care, and respect.

I don't know if it was because I had to wait so long, or just that I wanted it so badly, but I cherished every day with these two little children trusted to my care as their mother. I felt that God had lent them to me and it was my duty to "return them to Him," after He had so graciously and kindly—though many years later—answered my prayer. I figured the time was short and I had better make the most of it. Therefore, to spend an entire day holding and rocking, or holding and reading to one or both of them was not unusual. It just seemed that I had to make up for lost time.

I was often asked, "Are they brother and sister?" "My, they favor you enough to be yours!" "Do they know they're adopted?" "Do you know their mothers?" These types of questions from others persistently plagued me. At first, I considered the questions were asked in innocence; then as time advanced, I considered the questions rude and thoughtless. My answers became: "Of course they are brother and sister." "They are mine!" "They know that they were chosen and not taken by chance," and of course, "I am their mother, and yes, I do know me!"

I am sure that children hear their parents talking of adoption and they cannot understand it. Our children understood about adoption better than most adults did, as there became more and more adopted children in our families through the years. They thought that adoption was the natural way to get a child; birth was just another option. But never was their understanding of it more evident than one day when it was raining outside and my son, Roger wanted to have the little boy across the street come over and play.

Because it was raining, I raised the garage door and the little boy rode his tricycle over, and the two rode their trikes around and around the garage floor. I peeped out the door every so often to see that all was okay. At lunchtime, I stepped out to take them some sandwiches, and as I opened the door, I heard the neighborhood boy say to Roger, "Hey! Roger, you know what? She's not your mother!"

I told Steve it was time for him to go home and as he rode out on his tricycle, I lowered the garage door, leaned my sorrowful shoulders against the door, and wept, momentarily forgetting about the precious overall-clad, three-year-old boy standing beside me. I felt a soft tug on my apron and two little arms folded around my leg.

I looked down at the soft, gentle eyes and heard my little boy say, "Don't cry, Mommy, he just meant that I didn't grow in your stomach!"

I gathered up the child into my arms and hugged him until I could hug him no more. What wisdom! What a blessing! And I had grumbled for waiting so long for a child, thinking God had forgotten me! Just looking at what He had given me for waiting caused such a surge of thankfulness that I was left limp and weak. Surely good things DO come to those that wait!

When Lucinda's friends came over when she was in kindergarten, I heard one of them say to her, "I wish I could be adopted just like you!" Once, one of her friends asked me if I would please adopt her, too. Time brought many good things, and these children growing up, secure in the knowledge that they were loved and wanted was a good thing.

MAGNET MESSAGE:

"The little boy You gave me so long ago, Dear Father, has never disappointed me. He has given us so much of himself in devotion to not only us, but to You. The wisdom of the little guy at such an early age always amazed and astounded me. Thank you for him, for his life, and all he has come to mean to us, his parents." In Jesus Name, Amen

"Even a child is known by his doings, whether his works be pure, and whether they be right." Proverbs 20:11

77. The Lost Cap

It was a darling cap. It was hand-knit with white angora fur around the face. Attached to the soft peak at the top was a little ball of angora fuzz, and strings tied the cap securely under the chin.

Our little girl was six years old when we purchased the cap to go with the matching sweater. Because of her sensitivity to cold, we always made sure she never left the house in the winter without her cap on her head. She was very susceptible to ear aches, and this helped prevent them.

But. . . she hated that little cap. She thought of every reason in the world not to wear it. Once when she had used all of the excuses she could think of, she simply hid it.

One morning the school bus honked for her in front of the house. (If any of the children were not waiting in their regular spot, the driver would honk until either the child came out or a mother waved him on.)

That particular morning, we were again searching for that cap! "But I didn't hide it last night," Lucinda wailed pitifully. "I'm sorry, I don't believe you," I said. "You hid it once before, so why should I not think you've hidden it again?"

Exasperated, I hurried her out the door to the waiting bus. Calling after her, I shouted, "Don't cry to me tonight when you have one of your awful ear aches!"

Furious with her, I closed the door and as the bus drove away, I gathered the laundry on the way to the utility room. My anger toward her built. I felt she knew exactly where the cap was and just wouldn't tell me. Muttering to myself, I opened the machine lid to throw in the laundry and there it was--The Cap! In the washing machine where I had put it the night before, intending to wash it before she wore it again.

How ashamed I felt. What was I to do? I must make it up to her. I paced the floor watching the clock. It would be 9:15 before the first recess. Could I wait that long to tell her how sorry I was?

At 9:00, I drove up to Mustang Elementary and parked by the playground. I waited. Finally, the bell rang, and the first graders streamed out for recess. It wasn't long until I saw that long, red hair gleaming in the sunlight. There she was!

I stepped from the car and called to her. Her little face lit up when she saw me and she bounced to the car. "It's Mommy!" she squealed to her friends who followed her over to me. She threw her little arms around my neck, genuinely glad to see me.

"Oh, Lucinda," I cried. "I am so sorry. I found your cap where I had put it last night. Will you please forgive me for not believing you?"

She looked puzzled as she tried to remember what in the world I was talking about. She had forgotten the incident and I had re-opened it. We hugged and just as quickly as she had appeared, she disappeared back into the recess crowd.

Years later, as I was cleaning out her closet after she left home, I found some of the papers, notes, and assignments she had kept from her college classes. As I opened one of her old notebooks, I came across an assignment sheet that an English professor had given her. The instructions on it were to write a paper on some incident in your life and how it affected you.

Stapled to the sheet was the essay she had written when she had turned in the lesson. It was entitled, simply, "The Cap." The paper was written in its entirety about the angora cap episode when she was six years old. Across the top, the professor had written a glowing critique of the paper and marked it with an A-plus.

The final paragraph of the essay summed up the effect the cap incident had made on her life. It read:

". . . .and I learned that I had a mother who could not only admit it when she made a mistake, but would even apologize for it.. . ."

MAGNET MESSAGE:

Give us forgiving hearts so that we may expect forgiveness from You when we stray from Your presence. In Jesus' name, Amen.

"To err is human, to forgive, divine." Alexander Pope

78. Behind the Closet Door

When our daughter left home, ten years would pass by before I redecorated her room. I am afraid I am guilty of almost making it a shrine, because I just did not want to change a thing about it.

Finally, as it became necessary to make changes, I ended up storing some of her things in her closet with her promise to get them "someday." There were scrapbooks, mementos of her high school days, photos, books, and clothes, clothes, clothes.

But the things that especially caused me to spend many hours in her closet were the unexpected things I came across. With much nostalgia, I sat one day in her closet, sorting out things. ...and memories.

Hanging on the back rod, completely out of sight, I found her Camp Fire Girl ceremonial gown beaded with hundreds of beads. I recalled the long, hard work she put into beading it. There was the matching beaded headband on which she had beaded her Indian name, Ta-Wo-Kee, which meant "Great Book Teacher," and it was hung over the hook sealed in a plastic bag. Dangling across the hanger and tied together were her Indian moccasins, which completed the costume she wore when she enacted the Lord's Prayer in Indian sign language for the PTA when she was in the sixth grade.

Stored in the closet was a white organdy lace dress that she had worn her very first Easter Sunday when she was seven months old.

Her baby-doll, the Madam Alexander doll I got her for Christmas when she was five years old that said "Ma-Ma" when she was tilted over, was slung up on the top shelf of her closet. The doll brought back the memory of me climbing into the attic where I had hidden it before Christmas, and when I had accidentally turned her over, the sound of "Ma-Ma" had brought her running out of her room wanting to know "what that noise was."

There was the little dress I made her when she was three on which I had sewn my grandmother's tatting for trim, and there was a lovely little stuffed doll her grandmother Lemmons had made her when she was two.

There were music boxes, drawings, and notes and cards on which she had written to her "Purrrrr-fect Mother," and decorated them with pictures she had drawn of kittens. The "I love you, Mommy" cards, and her written prayers thanking God for "y'all 'dopting me" were piled neatly in a stack.

There were boxes filled with papers she brought home from kindergarten through first grade. As the years had gone by, the best papers had been saved from all the other grades. There were notes from her teacher saying what a polite and special little girl she was. One note told me about Lucinda telling her teacher that she "had to go home." When the teacher had asked her why, she remarked, "Because I promised myself I would not come to school ever again and my mommy taught me never to break a promise."

The most touching thing I found, though, was a worn and faded box. I recognized it immediately and I opened it.

Our children called my mother "Mother Dear," and I knew instantly the box contained a gift Mother Dear had given her on her 13th birthday. Inscribed in gold, and lettered in Old English print, were the words, Leaves of Gold. Next to the Bible, this was Mother's favorite book, and she felt there were so many good meditations in it, she often gave a copy of it to those she loved.

I opened the first page and in Mother's beautiful penmanship, she had written: "To my dear little granddaughter, Lucinda. Love from Mother Dear."

I closed the book. I closed the box. And I closed the door. But I could not close my heart. A part of it stayed behind the door.

MAGNET MESSAGE:

"I expect to pass through this world but once. Any good thing, therefore, that I can do or any kindness I can show to any fellow human being, let me do it now. Let me not defer nor neglect it, for I shall not pass this way again."(From Leaves of Gold)

"Take delight in the Lord and He shall give you the desires of your heart." Psalm 37:4

79. "Where will I go?"

O ur two precious children blessed our lives through the adoption process, and as they began to get older, we often talked of getting "another baby." I had hoped someday to be the mother of at least four children, so I am afraid I spent a good part of my time in filling out applications and sending them to as many places as possible. And when I wasn't doing that, I was constantly talking about it.

It was when our daughter was seven and our son was five that I began to worry about our son. I noticed that every time I talked of getting another baby, he became depressed and sad. Thinking it to be future sibling jealously, I would go into lectures of how he mustn't be selfish, that there were other babies to adopt and we would love them as much as we did him. His eyes would droop and he would look sadly into space.

I thought we were going to have a problem here with a child being self-centered and spoiled. I was to learn that I could never have been more wrong.

One Sunday morning after class, his Sunday School teacher told me that she, too, was worried about him. She said he was wistfully looking far away in class and she asked him what was wrong.

"I just wish my Mommy could get another baby so she would be happy," he told her.

That night as I tucked him in bed, he reached up and hugged me, holding tightly to my neck as if not to let go. "Mommy, I hope you get another baby soon," and he spoke very softly.

"Well, I do too, Roger. It will be nice to have another baby. I am glad that you want us to get another one."

I noticed tears glistening in his eyes as he asked me sadly, "Where will I go when you get another baby?" "What on earth are you talking about?" I asked. "You would not go anywhere. You are our son."

His lip quivering, he answered, "But Mommy, when Daddy gets another car, the other car goes away."

My heart broke. In his little boy mind, this precious child would have sacrificed his own happiness for mine.

MAGNET MESSAGE:

Time has proven, dear Father, just how very special this son You gave us, really is. We are so thankful for this gift as he has blessed our lives beyond all we could have hoped for. In Jesus' name, Amen.

"This is my beloved son, in whom I am well pleased..." Matthew 3:17

80. The Vanishing Camaro

I stood at the door and watched the black sports car slowly driven from my view. When the sight of it disappeared around the curve of the street, I brushed away the tears as I thought of the day I first saw it--and our son behind the wheel driving it into its prepared spot on the driveway.

He was sixteen years old, a new driver's license tucked safely in his billfold, and a darling spread-out grin on his still-a-little-boy face! He worked hard for that car. He saved every cent from his grocery-sacking job and paid cash for it. He continued to work long hours to earn money to "soup it up," pay the insurance, buy the fancy tires, repaint it, and of course, pay for its gas.

I remembered how, if he had any days off, he spent them with his head stuck under the hood of that beloved Camaro. In fact, the most familiar sight in the neighborhood had been the one of the black car, hood up with a pair of legs protruding out from under it, looking much like a black monster devouring a long-legged boy, head first!

I watched him "baby" that car through thick and thin. I watched him through the disappointment of learning his stereo system had been stolen. I cried for him when he slid off into a ditch during an ice storm, and hurt even more for him as he surveyed the damage.

By the time he entered college, the Camaro had been completely rebuilt: new engine, new inside and outside, and a new paint job. It was a classy car and he looked so sporty behind the wheel. I could always hear him coming home, and so could the neighbors! The muffler, coupled with the beat of his stereo, never failed to announce his arrival.

When he enrolled in college for his first year, he was amazed at the amount of gas it took to commute to his classes. The old Camaro got only eight miles to a gallon of gas, and his now part-time job just couldn't finance the cost.

Too sentimental to sell his cherished car, I watched as he "retired" it to the back yard, and covered it with a car cover. I watched him in his daily inspection of it as he sat quietly behind its wheel, reflecting on its memories and "testing its stereo."

That year he bought a little truck to drive to college that got better mileage so he could afford it, but it never held the place in his heart the Camaro held.

For several years the Camaro sat, like a rejected friend, in wind, rain and snow, alone in the back yard. Finally, he had to make a serious decision. He hoped to keep the old car for a son he might have some day, but expenses of college and his upcoming marriage made it necessary to sell it.

And now, as I stand at the door, I am so glad that he is not here to see the buyer of his boyhood dream drive it away. My "little boy memories" are now "grownup son realities." As the car passes from my view, so passes forever an exciting era in a young boy's life . . .

MAGNET MESSAGE:

Thank you for every memory of our children and every moment we spend with them. May we be blessed with many more to come. In Jesus' name, Amen.

"When I was a child, I talked like a child, I thought like a child, and I reasoned like a child. When I became a man, I put childish ways behind me." I Corinthians 13:11

81. If Rooms Could Talk

I stood in the hallway and looked into the now-vacant room, and I wondered, "If rooms could talk, what would this one say?"

". . . . . .A little boy grew to manhood within my walls. It was there by the door that his crib stood, and he drifted off to sleep to the beautiful strands of classical music.

"The baby soon outgrew his crib and it was replaced with a youth bed, and he was lulled to sleep to the lovely piano music of Roger Williams.

"All too soon, that bed was replaced by a super-sized water bed to accommodate his now-lanky body and long legs. By then, he was falling to sleep to the rock music of his peers.

"He spent time studying at the desk by my window while listening with earphones, to the music his parents did not want to hear. He strung wires all around my walls and over my door facings, hooking them behind nails he drove into my sheet rock. Underneath the layers of paint that built up with each new paint job, murals lie hidden that tell of each stage of his life. There is Snoopy on his house, Linus with his blanket, Star Wars characters, and finally, football symbols.

"At last, I was painted solid white once again, making room on my walls for posters and newspapers clippings to be thumb tacked into the newly-painted surface. Black smudges of fingerprints from newspaper print dotted the areas around posters and the light switch like little animal tracks. With the removal of one poster for another, the "tracks" smeared up my walls even more.

"I watched as his heart broke for the first time dealing with his first love. I shared with him those private moments of pain as he lay on his bed, gazing up at my ceiling where he had tacked deflated balloons ablaze with endearing messages that had lost their meaning.

"I enjoyed his music and it made me vibrate, but I welcomed the change that solitude brought when he pondered life's decisions and choices as he sat quietly at his desk, head in hands.

"I grew lonesome when he went to college. He was seldom within these walls of mine, but I was happy when he returned. My window shades were opened, flooding me with light, and his music returned with him.

"Sometimes he sang along with his music and it made me happy. I think I just sort of died when he married and left me permanently. My walls are stripped bare except for the nails, tacks, and the fingerprint smudges. I look around and I see these remnants of the boy who once lived, laughed, and cried within my walls:

"The tacks in the ceiling, the naked nails protruding from their vantage point above my door, now void of the electrical wires where stereo speakers once hung, the indentation in the carpet where the bed had been, the moisture rings on the desk where cans of pop once sat, the mildew spot on the carpet caused by wet towels being left too long in one spot, and the wastebasket full of gum and candy wrappers. All of these things

testify to the fact that a boy was grown here.

"The discarded Nikes, the stacks of comics, and the games for ages two to adult all lie on the closet floor, forgotten by time. A Cub Scout shirt with the den number patch on the sleeve, the embroidery raveling around the edges, hangs forlornly on the back rack of the closet.

"Yes, he is gone, but after a period of mourning, I will receive another coat of paint, new carpet, and new furniture. My walls will be repaired and the holes in them filled, and the cycle will begin again. I will gear up to receive another generation, maybe grandchildren who will again lighten me up and cause my walls to dance with happiness."

. . .and that is what this one room might say if it could talk. But it doesn't need to; it said it all silently as I stood and looked into its loneliness. I can feel the heart and soul of the precious son who grew up there and I am "hearing" every word the room is "saying."

MAGNET MESSAGE:

We have only one chance, Dear Father, to bring our children up in the knowledge of Your Word; please give us the patience and courage to never fail You on this. In Jesus' name, Amen.

"Correct thy son, and he shall give thee rest; yea, he shall give delight unto your soul." Proverbs 29:17

82. And the Tree Grew

The tree was a sprig, no larger than a pencil, when I pushed it down into the soft, moist soil in our back yard. During the years, it survived kittens jumping on it as it swayed in the gentle breezes; it even survived a brief encounter with the lawn mower, and somehow managed to grow into the magnificent tree it is today.

I walked around our yard one evening recently, and found myself reminiscing about that tree, and with each step I took, the large tree seemed to softly whisper each sweet memory to me.

I thought of the swing set that had been near the tree on which a little redheaded girl and her little brother had played. Underneath the swings, the worn-off grass was a testimony to the fact that a safe place for children to play was more important that a lush, green lawn with no bare spots.

And the tree grew. . .

I recalled the little wading pool where they splashed and cooled off during the hot summer days, the games of Star Trek they played for hours on end, and the back yard picnics we shared.

As I stepped over the stump of a plum tree, long ago cut down, I was reminded of the grave there beside it of their favorite cat, Luke. I thought of the many times they played with that cat and picked the plump, juicy, plums from off the tree. One time in particular I remembered was when they wanted to go to the circus. To earn the money for tickets, they picked plums, washed them, bagged them, and loaded them into their little red wagon. I watched them as they walked down the street, one pulling the wagon, the other behind, holding onto the top of the cargo so that the plum packages did not spill off.

How jubilant they were when after only twenty minutes or so, they returned with the empty wagon rattling behind them as they ran, squealing all the way, "We got $12.00!" When calls for more plums began pouring in, they picked, washed, bagged, and delivered more until they had earned enough to go to the circus and take friends with them!

And the tree grew. . .

As I strolled through where the blackberry patch had been, I could see the little boy with his beloved dog, Zap, patiently petting him beneath the tree that was, by now, tall enough to barely shade him.

I could see the little girl as she sat on the railroad ties used to separate the garden from the path, the cat in her arms. I remembered the complaints as they grumbled about picking blackberries "with all those stickers." Blackberry cobbler for supper-- and the stickers were soon forgotten. As I continued walking slowly around the yard, I could almost hear the groans from having to help pick beans and snap them, too.

And the tree grew. . .

I looked out over the back lot where that old garden had been when it provided our family with a bountiful harvest, and I could see once again the little boy in his overalls walking behind his father, his finger looped around the hammer hook on his daddy's overalls. Up and down each row he walked, placing his feet, one in front of the other, directly in the footprints of his father.

As I walked up toward the patio, I noticed again the chipped-out round holes in it. I thought of the little girl who chipped them out while jumping around on her pogo stick.

And the tree grew. . .

A small mound of dirt, long ago covered by grass still shows faintly where days were once spent building roads and ditches with Tonka toys.

I could see the young boy on the riding mower as he earned extra money, and I could see the little girl as she skipped and played, picking dandelions, her long hair gleaming like new copper in the sunlight.

And the tree grew. . .

Now that the tree was tall and strong, it no longer could sway or bend so easily. Its branches, now thick and sturdy, were ready to receive children to climb its trunk, hang up a swing, or even build a roomy tree house! By now, it cast its shadow completely over the yard and it towered many feet into the air.

I walked back up to the house, but as I paused to look again upward at the mighty tree, I thought about the evenings when, as the breeze rustled its leaves, it seemed to call to the children. Now it was strong and secure, and they could climb to their heart's content.

And the tree was grown.

But, alas! The children did not answer. Only the quietness of the yard and faint sounds of the past passed through the old tree's limbs. . .

The children were grown. . .

MAGNET MESSAGE:

May we "bend the twig" while there is time to shape the tree, and teach our children about You while their hearts are tender and easily molded. In Jesus' Name, Amen

"As for man, his days are like grass; as a flower of the field, so he flourishes. When the wind has passed over it, it is no more; and in its place acknowledges it no longer." Psalm 103:16

83. *Marriage Is a Permanent Condition*

The handsome young man sat alone at the jewelry counter, intently studying the glittering wedding sets under the glass before him. Oblivious to anyone else around him, it was obvious to others in the store that he knew exactly what he was looking for in a wedding set.

A salesman came to assist him, and after questioning the young man as to the price range and cut of diamond he wanted, brought out a large black velvet tray with loose stones and assorted mountings inserted in the narrow slots.

The young man, deep in thought, picked up different rings, turned them slowly around and around, asked for a jewelry loupe, looked closely at each one, only to put them back down again and again.

At last, the young shopper singled out a dainty gold band with places for channel-set diamonds. As he counted the possible amount of places stones could be set, he muttered half aloud and half to himself, "This one would be perfect for up to a twenty-five year band. I believe twenty-five would fit--one for each year."

"Excuse me," the salesman replied, and walked away only to return with another salesman.

"Would you repeat what you just said?" he asked, as he approached the young man who sat quietly, deep in thought.

Puzzled, he put down the ring and looking up, asked the salesman what he meant. "You said you thought the ring would be good as a twenty-five year anniversary ring by being large enough to accommodate twenty-five diamonds."

"That's right," he said. "It would fit just perfectly behind this engagement ring and he held up a marquise cut with more channel-set diamonds beside the center stone.

The salesmen, now leaning over the counter absorbed in this young man's statement, reacted with complete shock!

"This is a first for us," they replied. "We have worked as jewelry salesmen for many years, and most wedding sets are selected by both the bride and groom so they can agree together who will get the rings when they divorce. In fact, most have already signed a pre-nuptial contract about this before they come."

The man lowered his eyes as the salesman continued, "And here you are selecting the rings by yourself for the girl you hope to still be married to in twenty-five years! Son, do you know how rare you are?"

The handsome young man looked down at the rings he had selected and quietly and humbly replied, "But marriage is a permanent condition."

MAGNET MESSAGE:

Help us to return to being a nation of loving families with rock-solid marriages. In Jesus' name, Amen.

"....for this cause shall a man leave his father and mother and be united to his wife and the two shall be one flesh. So they are no longer two, but one. Therefore, what God joins together, let no man put asunder." Matthew 19:6

84. *Wherein Dwells Love*

I drove up to the big old farmhouse and sat silently in the car a moment before getting out. How different the house looked. It was hard to realize it was the same house that had stood proud, erect, and gleaming white in the sunlight when I was a child.

I scanned the tall weeds in the yard, looking for signs that an immaculately- groomed hedge once grew around it. I saw the remains of the magnificent pear tree that we had climbed as children to pick the pears for our grandmother, Mama-Dear, to can for the winter months.

Around the edge of the house's crumbling foundation, I saw the familiar iris. In their heyday, they were one huge bouquet of color. The bulbs, still in the ground, but long forgotten, were making their annual appearance. The slender stalks were pushing up through the weeds, the bulging buds ready to burst open, the only thing of beauty remaining in the yard. Stuck in the ground beside them was a rusty old spade, left there by the one who attended them for the last time.

I decided to take one last look through the old house whose walls once rang with the laughter of twenty-four grand-children! As I stepped over the concrete chunks and through the weeds, I recalled the happy times this old lawn had once known when children frolicked on its plush green grass, catch-

ing lightning bugs, playing ball, and eating "mountains of ice cream" that Mama-Dear made from the fruits of her trees.

I was so caught up in my memories of Mama-Dear and Pa-pa-Dear that I was only vaguely aware of the four-lane highway now running through the land Papa-Dear once farmed.

As I opened the rickety, hanging screen door, memories of an entire childhood engulfed me. I stepped onto the creaking porch and made my way into the living room of the old house.

My eyes danced quickly off the walls, to the floors, to the windows, taking in every delicious memory. Mama-Dear had a curio cabinet over in that corner, and I used to sit over there, I thought, and go through her collection of whatnots from around the world.

I walked on into the dining room and I could almost smell Mama-Dear's cooking. There is where her buffet stood, covered with all kinds of desserts. Against that wall over yonder was her china cabinet and in the middle of this room was that massive dining table that could easily seat fourteen of us around it. I used to bounce my basketball around that table, the vibrations on the hardwood floor causing the dishes in her china cabinet to rattle.

As my eyes darted around the room, I remembered how we cousins would congregate to whisper and giggle over which of our grown cousins had brought home the prettiest bride. We were all here at Christmas time, so we would "inspect" each girl and then vote on the one we liked best, starry-eyed over the thought of being a bride someday ourselves.

My eyes were misty by the time I wandered into the kitchen. A stepladder had been in a corner and I used to climb up on it to "help" Mama-Dear with the dishes. From the kitchen, I could see over into the sitting room and sun porch. I thought of time I spent there one hot summer under a fan as I recuperated from chicken pox. Papa-Dear, retired from farming, sat over by the window listening to his radio, the candy closet behind him. He always kept it stocked with orange slices for the grandchildren who came in and out daily.

I looked at the old fireplace and recalled the nights gathered around it waiting for Santa to appear.

The bedrooms were large to accommodate the big brass beds with their feather mattresses. We could get lost in those mattresses that Mama-Dear had stuffed with goose feathers, and we sank out of sight when we jumped into the middle of one.

I stepped out onto the back porch, and from there, I could see the skeletal remains of Mama-Dear's canning house, the collapsed garage, and the chinaberry trees.

Cousins chunking chinaberries at one another was painful. We picked our "ammunition" off the trees, chose up sides, and had a "fight." Mama-Dear's chinaberry trees were always stripped bare.

As I made my way back to the car, I turned for one last glance toward the place where I had enjoyed so many summers and Christmases as a little girl. The house looked forgotten and forlorn, but there had been a time when the happiness and love within its walls, had shaken the big old house with laughter and merriment.

Suddenly! A burst of color caught my eye! One lonely little iris had opened during the time I stepped inside, and it seemed to call to me .I quickly ran back, grabbed the rusty spade, dug a few of the bulbs, and tucked them into the trunk of my car.

And now when I plant them in my own yard, Mama-Dear's flowers, like her home "wherein dwells love," will continue to thrive for generations yet to come.

MAGNET MESSAGE:

Heavenly Father, when we realize how short life really is, help us to savor every moment, to be happy in the time given us and to give You the glory. In Jesus' name. Amen.

"....and I will dwell in the house of the Lord forever." Psalm 23

85. "Where'd we get these dishes?"

"Go up into the attic, Belle, and bring down that big cardboard box," Daddy told me one day during the time after he had become legally blind and Mother was no longer at home.

I pulled down the retractable stairs and climbed up to the musty storage space above the garage. A quick glance revealed many memories: my baby sisters' crib, a rocker, filing cabinets, an old Underwood typewriter, a brass bed, and boxes, everywhere!

"Which one?" I called down to Daddy.

"The one marked "miscellaneous," he shouted, calling on a long ago remembrance of when he had put it up there.

I lugged the big box down the stairs and plopped it down on the kitchen table. It rattled with sound of dishes and silverware.

I brushed off the dust, and opened the flap. Instantly, I was a little girl again as I peered into its contents. The dishes were old, chipped, cracked and yellowed with time, but undeniably, they were the same dishes which we five, as children, had eaten from.

There were no two dishes alike. I recalled how when we were small, Mother used to wish for the day she would have a completely matching set of dishes. There was the plain, white plate my brother always insisted on having. He did not like his food on "flowers" or "printed junk," because he said "it didn't taste right."

My older sister had to have the divided plate. She didn't like for her food to "touch," and she spread each little item in separate piles and ate one food at a time.

I didn't care if my food got mixed. It all got to the same place, anyway, but I did like for it to be on the plate with the dainty, printed blue flowers. It made it taste better.

We always had so much company for dinner, especially after church on Sunday, and I remembered how Mother used to say her dream for those special dinners was to be able to set a table where all the dishes matched. When we had a lot of people over, she would borrow matching plates from her good friend and neighbor next door. And it never failed, when we sat down to Sunday dinner, one of us would pick up a plate, inspect it, turn it over and say, "Hey, Mother, where'd we get these dishes?" Our embarrassed mother would simply smile and change the subject.

When we grew up, we got Mother a set of Damask Rose Noritake China, and I recall how thrilled she was to finally have a matching set of dishes. She always said she loved to set "a pretty table." I think she appreciated that gift more than anything we ever gave her. She always told us the only gift she ever wanted from us was "for you all to be Christians," but we believe those dishes ran a close second.

I rummaged on down to the bottom of the box sitting on the kitchen table, and found the tarnished silver-plated forks and spoons. We all had our favorite fork and spoon back then, too, and none of those matched either.

I picked up the one with hearts and flowers on the handle that had been mine, and examined carefully the now-worn-smooth design, thinking of all the memories that one old spoon brought back. I used to run in from school, grab that spoon, and scoop out a big pile of brown sugar, run out the door with it in one hand, and my bouncing basketball in the other. For some strange reason, I pretended I was eating sand.

It was also the spoon I used to pour myself a taste of vanilla one day when Mother was baking. Vanilla smelled so good; shouldn't it taste good, too? I got the shock of my life when I put that spoon to my lips that day. I never tried that again.

"If you want anything in there, Belle, go ahead and take it," Daddy was saying as he interrupted my thoughts.

"Anything of value?" Just priceless pieces of my cherished childhood, I thought. No amount of money in the world could buy any of these treasures. I took the dishes, washed them, packed them safely back into the box, and I know that not one of us will ever ask, "Where'd we get these dishes?" We know.

 MAGNET MESSAGE:

Dear Father in Heaven, I am forever grateful for the example, love and devotion, and all the sacrifices our parents always made for us. I just pray with all my heart that they know what they mean to us. In Jesus' name, Amen.

"And all thy children shall be taught of the Lord; and great shall be the peace of thy children." Isaiah 54:1

86. The Last House Daddy Built

The first house daddy built was in 1933, and he built it for Mother's wedding present. The last one he built was for her, too, in 1968. Night after night, he sat at his drawing board designing the home as he thought she wanted it to be. He planned on this being their final home. He was getting ready to retire and had purchased two acres in Mustang, Oklahoma and was "raring to get started" doing the thing he loved best—building a house.

"Just so I have a big kitchen and a big dining area is all I want to request," Mother told him. "You design the rest."

And design he did. He put everything together so that a short hall was the only "wasted" space—as he called it—in the entire house. The house had only nine windows, but bookcases were to line the living room walls, and plenty of space for lounging around the fireplace, and her precious kitchen would display thirty cabinets.

Daddy bought his black horn-rimmed magnifying glasses at the TG&Y for $1.00. He hung them near the end of his nose and whistled away as he drew on those plans. I looked over his shoulder from time to time when we went to visit them, and I watched him laboriously draw in each electrical plug and vent. He had a plan for everything and a place for each item. I knew this was a labor of love, plain and simple.

After he got off work, Daddy traveled every evening out to Mustang to work on their home. He dug the foundation by hand, twice the depth that was required by FHA. We went out one evening to see the progress and as we drove up, Daddy was down in the ditch, and dirt was just a-flying out of it! He was digging and whistling.

"This house will be here long after I'm gone, Belle," he sang out, "I'm building it to LAST!"

And that is exactly what he always did. Every house he built in Oklahoma City while I was growing up was truly a masterpiece and work of art. He put his whole heart into every house he built, and his cabinetwork was as much a beautiful example of his artistry as the house itself was. He told my little brother that there wasn't a day in his life that he didn't want to go work. I knew that was true, because he always whistled. He whistled when he filed his saw, he whistled when he hammered, and he left in the mornings whistling and came home from work, whistling. Mother told him one day he acted like he owned the world! "My Father does, he replied!"

When he finally got the frame up on the Mustang home and the walls in, he began to spend the night on the floor during the weekends so he could work late into the night. Mother came out and brought his supper and helped him.

I went over one night and he was putting in the insulation. He was putting twice as much as required. "This house will be tight as a drum," he told me, "The heating bill will be as low as possible because no air will escape." The house was built to be as economical and sturdy as it was attractive.

We all watched with great interest as he put on the final

touches. He got on the roof to put on the shingles and his neighbor called out: "Morris Rogers, I've noticed you put about 10 nails to a shingle; your house is a living lightning rod!" And that was the truth! Everything IN or ON the house was made to stay PUT!

When OG&E laid a pipeline near the house, they filled up his drainage ditch with dirt. Daddy told them if it rained, it would flood the house. "I didn't dig that ditch for nothing!" he told the linemen.

Needless to say, a hard rain came before Daddy could get it re-dug and it flooded the utility room and adjoining bath and bedroom. The insurance company came out and gave him an estimate for the damage. They wanted to completely re-carpet the bedroom, but Daddy said, "No need to do THAT, it only ruined the closet carpet—just cut a piece to fit in there, and that is all you need to pay for. They tried to tell him he was eligible for the entire room but Daddy just said, "Nope, that's why our insurance premiums are so high!"

Another time when a pipe broke in the shower and he had the man come out to fix it, they had to take out the tile and rebuild the shower. As the man worked, I dropped by to see the folks. I went in the bathroom where the tile man was working, and he was grumbling and muttering to himself. "I'd like to know WHO built this house. I've never had such a hard time tearing out something as I have here. This house is built to outlast ME!" And he swore under his breath. I cleared my throat and told him I'd be glad for him to meet the man who built it. I called Daddy in there and said, "Here is my father; he built this house!"

The tile man apologized all over the place and ended up telling Daddy if he ever built a house, he knew whom he'd have build it.

The finished house was the gathering place of all our families and the fireplace was the focal point of the whole house. It was the coziest we ever felt. When we all came home for Christmas, we had to open all the windows and the front and back doors because the room would be so hot. I have never again seen a fireplace like that one; one that held in the heat and kept it in the house. None seemed to escape from the chimney. They didn't need any "artificial" heat in the winter if they just lit the fireplace. When we all gathered there, the walls inside it rang with laughter and the merriment comparable only to that I had experienced at my grandparents' house as a child.

Outside the house, Daddy planted a garden on about 1/2 acre. He also planted fruit trees, pecan trees and grapevines. He had might near the most beautiful garden in town. The rows were ramrod straight made that way by strings that he carefully stretched across each row to have a guide to follow. He worked in the garden all summer long and Mother filled the freezer with the bounty from it. Come winter, he shelled pecans until his hands stained brown, and Mother made pecan pies and froze the pecans for Christmas candies. It was a beautiful season of my heart as I watched my beloved parents enjoy the fruits of their labors and reap the rewards of lives well lived.

MAGNET MESSAGE:

Thank you, dear Father, for all the memories we enjoy of the lives lived in the house on Sara Road in Mustang, Oklahoma, the last house Daddy built. Built not with just nails and a hammer, but with love and devotion to Mother, and to us, his children, and love and devotion for You, too. Nothing showy or pretentious, the house represented the life he lived—humble and honest—and by example, he taught us all that was required to be Your Children, too. In Jesus' Name, Amen

"Except the Lord build the house, they labor in vain who build it…." Psalms 127

87. The Porch Swing

The split and splintered slats, the rusty chains dangling, were piled on top of the garbage can awaiting the trash collector.

It was early that morning that I stepped out on the porch and glancing upward, saw the two heavy, steel hooks still protruding from the ceiling where once the old porch swing had hung.

A forlorn and forgotten aura surrounded the broken swing as it sat silently on the trash heap, silhouetted against the brightness of the rising sun. It caused a sadness to stir within me as I thought of the secrets that old swing must surely know.

I was standing on the front porch of my parents' home that day as I watched the trash collectors sling the remnants of the swing onto the truck and drive off. I watched the truck until it was out of sight, and I couldn't keep from thinking what that old swing had meant to me.

Daddy had hung the swing on the porch the first year they had moved into the house he built just before he retired. All of us were grown by then, but we were always bringing back our own children who loved to play on the swing.

As the years rolled by, seventeen grandchildren would, at one time or another, be rocked to sleep by that swing, lulled by

the rhythm of the clicking chain with each sway.

It could soothe the crying baby, entertain a giggly toddler, frame a young romantic couple's evening under the stars, or calm the troubled soul of a weary adult.

But most of all, I remember it being the spot where my best friend---Mother---and I always sat during the gentle spring evenings and hot summer nights.

Recipes were exchanged, problems solved, tears dried, joys remembered, secrets shared, hopes realized, and plans made, all to the breezy sway of a little bench hanging by two chains from the porch ceiling.

The old swing was a comfortable place to sit while we snapped beans, shelled peas, and peeled fruit for freezing.

Not long before the morning that the swing was towed away, Mother suffered several strokes that left her unable to ever again join me on the front porch swing for our evening visits. It was then we began to notice how time and weather had eroded the old swing's chains.

It was as if the swing sensed the dear lady's absence, and creaking with sadness, had simply folded itself up and died.

The swing was never replaced, and the empty hooks on the porch ceiling remain intact today. When I looked back at those hooks, I thought:

Perhaps some future owner of the house will someday hang another swing from those hooks and it will again sparkle with new life around it, rewarding someone else with its joys---joys that for me have now passed forever into precious memories.

MAGNET MESSAGE:

In sadness, Father, we often learn more about You, Your Goodness, and Your love for us. In Jesus' name, Amen.

"...a God ready to pardon, gracious and merciful, slow to anger, and of great kindness." Nehemiah 9:17

88. My Best Friend

Since she married before I did, she could give me excellent advice. Because she was a parent long before I was, she could speak from experience on how to raise children. My best friend.

We spent long hours visiting with one another on every subject anyone could name. We didn't always agree, but we always cared for each other. My best friend.

She taught me to pray. To forgive. To be kind and to live in peace as much as lay within me to do so. She knew all about me, yet she continued to love me. My best friend.

She could criticize me and I knew it was done out of love and not malice. She was generous beyond belief, and totally and completely unselfish. She would have given her life for me. My best friend.

Her honesty, hospitality, and her cheerful heart were constant reminders of her total goodness. We sometimes hurt one another, but apologies and forgiveness always followed. We never held grudges. My best friend.

When I got in a bind, she was first to help. If I got blue and depressed, she was first to cheer. She was a faithful friend, a constant source of strength, and I never had to wonder how I stood with her. My best friend.

She taught me what is important in life. She gave me hope. She made sure that I was familiar with God's Word, and she made me aware of the consequences of going against that

Word. My best friend.

Then the time came that I should try to repay her for all she did for me. I tried to return to her the blessings she gave to me, but I fell miserably short. My best friend.

I stood helplessly beside her as the last vein collapsed and the IV's were removed. I watched sadly as her life slowly slipped from me after she whispered "yes" when I asked her if she was glad to see me. My best friend.

I held her as she died. I kissed the cold cheek good-bye, and I will miss her until eternity. My best friend.

If I could only tell her one more time how much I love and appreciate her, how precious the memories are that I have of her, and that I wish I could hug her just one more time. My best friend.

Sunday, I placed the roses on her grave. My first Mother's Day without her. My best friend.

MAGNET MESSAGE:

If I live long enough, Dear God, other Mother's Days will follow, and I know that every year will be just as difficult as this, the first one has been. Give me the courage to face them. Please. In Jesus' name, Amen.

"A friend loves at all times." Proverbs 17:17

89. What Kind of Mother Was This, Anyhow

She made the word "Mother" bring out such beautiful feelings within me when I was a child, that I couldn't wait to grow up and be one. She showed us that "Mother" was a word synonymous with depth of character and deep convictions. It represented someone who was pure and good during a time when men wore the pants, women wore the earrings and ponytails, men made the living, and women made the living worthwhile.

The morals, values, and Biblical truths that Mother taught us were taught by not only the word, but by deed as well. Whatever went for them went for us, as well.

What kind of mother was this, anyhow?

Mother never taught us that something was wrong while privately participating in that activity herself. We knew kids at school who would be in big trouble at home if they were caught trying alcoholic beverages, yet these same kids would often find their mothers prostrate with drunkenness when they got home from school. This made them terribly confused. They often told us how "lucky" we were to have parents who were not hypocrites.

What kind of mother was this, anyhow?

Mother insisted on sending us off to school every morning with eggs, toast, hot Ovaltine, bacon, and orange juice under our belts while other kids got to have a Snickers and a Coke. As we ran out the door to catch the school bus, each of us grabbed a lunch sack sitting on the kitchen counter next to Daddy's lunch pail and jug of iced tea. We never questioned how the lunches got there or how that big breakfast got on the table. They were just there. Always. Every morning.

What kind of mother was this, anyhow?

WE always had to be home from a date by 11:00 pm.; other kids got to stay out as late as they wanted. When we had something come up that would cause us to be late, we were required to call home. How embarrassing! Nobody else had to call their parents and report in like some kind of baby or something, but WE did. The other kids got to come and go as they pleased, and their mothers didn't wait up for them! Mother always said she couldn't close her eyes until we were all safely in the house.

What kind of mother was this, anyhow?

We were told if we got into trouble at school, we would get into worse trouble when we got home. "The teacher," she would say, "is always right." Other mothers would stomp to school and battle the teacher in front of their child, and we would wail that those mothers love their children! Mother was not impressed. She was totally unmoved by our emotional outbursts, and she never budged or compromised on one of her firm decisions. She was strong and confident and her NO meant just that. If the question had an answer that could possibly be YES, she weighed carefully all of the circumstances before committing herself, because once committed, she did not ever reverse her decision. This consistency, we learned, built security and stability into us and taught us that Mother was a trusted friend.

What kind of mother was this, anyhow?

She never let us do what the crowd was doing and did not care if she was unpopular with our friends. She said, "You will do right regardless of what everybody else does." She also had to know all about our friends. She had to know just everything! She had to know where we were going at all times, with whom we were going, and she would even tell us when to get back! The very idea! She was nosy, all right, and we couldn't run with just "anybody."

What kind of mother was this, anyhow?

We had to earn our money, and then Mother proceeded to tell us how to spend it! Other kids got an allowance to spend any way they chose. We had to take a certain percentage off the top for the contribution plate on Sunday. With the rest, we had to pay for necessities, save a part, and IF any was left over, we could "waste" it on a funny book or a Saturday afternoon picture show.

While growing up, we sometimes fail to reach a solid appreciation of the live-in treasure that blesses our home in the form of Mother. It sometimes takes becoming a mother yourself to realize how much love and hard work goes into being the kind of mother we had. How much easier it would have been for her to relax and go about her business without the constant effort of "staying on top" of all the hundreds of emotions, desires, whims, and changing moods of babies, then toddlers, then teens, and finally, adult children.

What kind of mother was this, anyhow?

Edgar A. Guest wrote a poem that was Mother's favorite, which she quoted to us all of our lives:

"I'd rather see a sermon, than hear one, any day,

"I'd rather someone show me, than merely point the way..."

Well, Mother you were "that kind of Mother, anyhow." We not only SAW your sermons, but we HEARD them, too. I am sure there were times, however, you must have felt we were both blind and deaf! What kind of Mother were you? Just the dearest in all the world, that's the kind. Thank you for everything! HAPPY MOTHER'S DAY!

This was my column for Mother's Day honoring my mother in May 1995.

90. *"There's My Apron!"*

When children, having been blessed by godly parents, have grown, and payback time comes around, siblings are often called upon to make the cruelest of life's decisions.

At a time when parents should be enjoyed by grandchildren, and appreciated by their grown children, these decisions can numb the mind and break the heart.

The saddest day of my life came when we could no longer provide proper care for our mother and we made the decision for her to enter a nursing home facility.

All of our lives, Mother gave of herself. Her family was her first priority, and she called her four daughters, her "precious jewels," and her one son, her "pride and joy." She was known for her delicious dinners, and her kitchen was the heart of our home.

My dearest memories of Mother are of her standing in front of the stove, her starched apron tied securely around her crisp housedress. The apron was always a focal point in her kitchen as it hung over the rack next to the stove, patiently awaiting the beginning of the next meal.

Mother's kitchen cabinet drawers were filled to the brim with her handwritten recipes. Although there was no organized recipe box, she could easily find just which one she wanted by looking for a chocolate smear, or a greasy butter smudge that usually blotched the paper of a well-used recipe. She often had me search for her Orange Slice Cake recipe, and I had only to look for the crinkled-up paper with the orange juice stain on it.

Her kitchen always smelled good and was a warm welcome to anyone visiting, as well as a comfort zone to us during stressful times.

We decided to bring Mother home for an afternoon visit to celebrate her 84th birthday. It had been fourteen months since she left the hospital to go straight into the nursing facility, and during that time, she had asked to see her home again. Worried that she would not want to return to the nursing home, we decided to take that chance anyway. We rented a van with a handicap lift on it, and I rode in it with her the twenty miles to her house. I answered all of her questions on the way.

"Did I teach school in Mustang?" "Yes, Mother, you did." "I don't remember it being so far away. Nothing looks familiar." The van reached the house. "Is this where I lived? It doesn't look like I thought it did."

I rolled her wheelchair into the living room, and she became a little girl in a wonderland. The many cross-stitched samplers on the wall caught her eye. The look of questions and wonders on her face showed the deep concentration going on in her mind trying to recall them. "Are all of those mine?" she asked over and over.

Two scriptures Mother had painted on plaques years ago still hung on the wall as she had left them. One Scripture is "If God be for us, who can be against us?" (Romans 8:31), and the other is, "I have no greater joy than to hear that my children walk in truth" (3 John 4).

"Where did I get those?" she asked.

As I rolled her wheelchair through each room, she studied the pictures and poems on the walls, and pictures of her grandchildren made her smile. The gong of the 85-year-old oak clock triggered a thoughtful glance toward where it sat on the mantel.

"Roll me into the kitchen...I want to see it," she told me. As I wheeled the chair into her kitchen, her face lit up, much like you would see a child's face light up at seeing Disney World for the first time!

"There's my apron!" she exclaimed, beaming. And she raised her hand and pointed to the towel rack by the stove where the limp and forgotten cloth still hung. It was truly fitting that after all of the meals the dear lady had cooked, the one thing that provided her mind with "instant recall" of happy memories was the sight of her beloved apron!

As we sat on the front porch waiting for the van to return, she said, "Daddy, this is all beginning to come back. I lived here, didn't I?" "Yes," he said "for 28 years."

Once back in the van for the return trip, I again rode with her and it was then that I had to hide my tears.

"Didn't we have a good day?" she said. "Yes, Mother, we did. Would you like to do this again?"

"Well, not today, but yes, another day." She was very tired but content. She had been "home" again and sixteen people had come by to eat lunch with her and to wish her a happy birthday. For a few short hours, she was our mother again, seated at the table, concerned about everybody getting enough to eat, and in her rightful place where she will always belong.

MAGNET MESSAGE:

Thank you for today, God, and each day we live in Your presence. Make us aware of Your many blessings. In Jesus' name, Amen.

"Who can find a virtuous woman for her price is far above rubies..." Proverbs 31:10

"I consider the days of old, I remember the years long ago..." Psalm 77:5

91. *Last Days Memories*

Anyone who entered Mother's hospital room, as she lay critically ill, might have accused her children of being disrespectful, but we knew we were behaving exactly as Mother would have wished. There would be plenty of time for tears, but they wouldn't fall where she could see them.

We gathered around her bed, and not fully realizing exactly how much of the conversation she comprehended, we decided to talk of the many things that made her such a good mother and what those things had meant to us.

Every sentence began with "Remember that time, Mother..." and each of us told of some special incident remembered that caused us to appreciate her so very much. A close look into her questioning eyes sometimes revealed what she could not say but helped us to know that she understood much of what we were saying. If this is so, then Mother died with the knowledge that her five children loved her dearly.

One of the nurses, in fact, was heard to say the night Mother died, "She lived as long as she did because she felt such love."

As each of us brought up a memory in the room that night, our brother, Bob, said, "I want to tell you what the worse thing I remember happening to me as a child!"

We all wondered what in the world he would say. He continued, and bending over Mother, he said, "Mother, do you remember that time I had an upset stomach and you sent Molly Lou to the store to get me a 7-Up? Well, she shook it all the way home and when I opened it, it spewed all over me. I was furious! To this day, it makes me mad and I remember it as the worse day of my life when I was small."

I was just sure I saw a smile cross Mother's lips, ever so slightly, but it was there. And happy her heart must have felt to know that the spilling of a 7-Up was the worst thing in his childhood that he could remember.

We each spoke of many things that night, and Mother went to sleep. It wasn't long afterwards that she passed from this life, and gone were the opportunities to tell her again of the many reasons we loved her so much.

I am grateful for the opportunities we had. As I slip into her robe every night, I can still smell the sweet fragrance of Estee Lauder Youth Dew Oil, which has surrounded her presence with its clean fragrance for over forty years, and now permeates all of her clothing. For me the aroma is comforting, and I am told that in time, it will help to heal. I keep waiting for that day.

 ## MAGNET MESSAGE:

I do not doubt her whereabouts, Dear God, but the sadness I feel is in the memories of her final days, what she wanted to say but couldn't and what I HOPE she understood me to say. I just wish every child could have a mother like ours. In Jesus' name, Amen.

"The memory of the just is blessed..." Proverbs 10:7

92. *"It's a deal!"*

I t's a deal!" were the last words Mother ever spoke. She lay in the emergency room suffering dehydration and the effects of yet another stroke, while awaiting her attending physician.

She had not spoken nor had she been able to move since first becoming so ill that hospitalization was required. Along with Daddy and all of us children, Mother's best friends and their daughter Angela--who was soon to be married--were there with me.

"Remember, now Polly, "Angela said to Mother as she peered directly into her face, "I expect you to be at my wedding in February."

Just as plain as day, Mother replied, "It's a deal!" We all beamed. This was a good sign. Mother had always managed to beat her brushes with death; she would beat it this time, too, and that positive statement reassured us.

But it was not to be. Mother never spoke again. She got weaker and weaker until there were no more veins to feed, and the doctor asked permission to shut off the IV feedings stating the brain damage was so extensive, that among other things, she would never be able to swallow. The alternative was a tube in the stomach with no guarantee that she was strong enough to withstand the surgery necessary to put it in. The second saddest day of my life came when that realization hit me. It was as though someone opened my chest and ripped out my heart.

In the next five weeks, I sat beside her bed and watched my dearest friend on this earth slowly slip from me. I talked with her as if she knew and understood everything I was saying, just as we used to sit on her porch swing and talk for hours. Only this time, I was to do all of the talking, as she could no longer be my faithful advisor, friend, and source of strength and wisdom.

I told her of many things: what a wonderful mother she always was. Even when she made us eat a big breakfast every morning when all the other kids got to have Cokes and candy. I told her how thankful I was that she never let our sassing get her down, always staying true to the decisions she made that kept us from harm's way.

I told her how grateful I was that she loved Daddy so much and showed it by always being sure his needs were met. I appreciated her always shielding him from everyday worries, which she would handle if she could.

I reminded her of the warm and cozy atmosphere she always provided for us. How I loved to skip home from school and have her there, the house smelling of good things.

I spoke to her about my difficult teen years when she never let me whine or feel sorry for myself, but insisted that I do what was right regardless of what the others did. "If the crowd jumped into a fire, would you?" she often asked me.

I reminded her of how many times I had heard her say to Daddy, "Didn't we do good?" and how they would laugh as they recalled their years together.

Toward the end of the five weeks, Mother began to get very cold...and clammy. I climbed into the hospital bed with her to try to keep her warm but it was impossible. "Mother," I whispered one evening, "You're going Home...I wish I could go with you." She fixed her eyes on the ceiling and opened them very wide.

It had been a long time since I had seen Mother's eyes that blue. The pupils were tiny, the size of pinheads, and the color was bright, clear, and as blue as the bluebonnets of Texas that she loved so dearly. During the duration of her illness that had begun about five years before, I had never seen the blue of her eyes. Strokes left the pupils permanently dilated so that the narrow rim of blue around them was barely noticeable.

But not now. She was her beautiful self as she always used to be, and I could not remove her fixation from the ceiling. Did she see angels? She held that look for several hours, never blinking, all the while breathing easily and peacefully. When the nurse came to turn her, she closed the blue eyes forever.

I continued to talk to her as I held her hand and laid my face against hers. "Mother," I said, "I love you so very, very, much." Her mouth closed and the next breath did not come. I reached under her shoulders, pulled her to me, and hugged her. With that, she sighed, and expelled her last breath. At that moment, she flushed warm and pink all over and a peace "that passes understanding" washed over her being. She was as beautiful in death as she had been all of her life. It was January 16, 1997--almost 35 years to the day that she had sat by her mother's side at the hospital and hugged her goodbye.

At the wedding in February, Angela had a screen set up in the front of the church building, and slides of the young couple flicked across it during the seating of the guests. As I was ushered in, I glanced up at the screen and saw a picture of my dear

mother, face smiling and beaming down at the wedding about to begin. Angela had found it among her photos and had made it into a slide, so that Mother could, indeed, be there.

When Mother had said, "It's a deal!" that is exactly what she meant!

MAGNET MESSAGE:

I watched Mother die, dear God, and was able to tell her of many things during those extra few weeks that I was given with her. Thank You for allowing me that extra special favor that gave me the peace I needed and the time to love her, literally, "to death." In Jesus' Name, Amen

"A virtuous woman is a crown to her husband..." Proverbs 12:4

93. *Daddy's Request*

I grew up during the 1950's when bleaching your hair was the big thing, especially within the teen-aged community. But my parents grew up in a time when a 'lady' did not color her hair.

"The Lord gave you beautiful hair, don't ever change it," was Mother's admonition. And Daddy was just as adamant about it, too. From their era, they viewed a woman with dyed hair in the same way we would later view a girl from our era with pierced ears!

When Mother died in 1997 after a bout of ill health, she and Daddy had been married sixty-four years. Lost and alone, Daddy became blind, and at ninety-four years of age, had to sell his house and move to an assisted living apartment. It was then, that with great caution, I decided to see if "blonds have more fun."

Well, although my conscience was slightly disturbed, I chose to take a chance. "After all," I reasoned, "My parents will never know." Mother was gone home, and Daddy couldn't even see it ….I was a grown woman and could make my own choices, couldn't I? Couldn't I? After all, it had been thirty-five years since I had tried the jet-black hair dye at age thirty!

I made the big change and a few weeks after I became a blond, Daddy fell gravely ill. Even though he was ninety-four years old and blind, his mind was sharp and witty, his words full of quips and wisdom. But systems were just shutting down from being just "plain ole tired," he told me, chuckling.

"Belle, I nearly died last night, and you know what? It was a wonderful feeling; nothing hurt, and all was peace and beauty. I don't know why anyone would fear death."

They called me at work that day to come quickly; he was sinking fast. I couldn't believe my ears since I had sat and visited with him only a couple of days beforehand. In fact, when I started to leave and said, "Bye, Daddy," He said, "Oh, Is that YOU, Belle?"

"Who did you think it was, Daddy?"

"I didn't know. I was just playing along, but now that I know it's you, sit back down and stay awhile longer."

Sometimes he couldn't recognize my voice too well, as his hearing had gotten worse, too.

Arriving in his room that day in February 2002, I could hear his breathing before I ever went in his room. I bent over to kiss him, and he said, "Belle, what have you done to your hair?" My heart skipped a beat—to respect him all these years—I am well into my sixties—and then to disappoint him in death broke my heart. I suddenly remembered how doctors say that near the end, the ears are sharpened and the sight becomes keen.

"Daddy, do you mean you can see my hair?"

"I shore can."

"What does it look like to you?"

"It looks like white fuzz, and I'll bet your mother is having a wall-eyed fit. I believe if I were you, I'd put it back."

I kissed Daddy goodbye and those were the last words he ever spoke.

I "put my hair back" the next week.

MAGNET MESSAGE:

I am so grateful for the man I had for my father on this Earth for sixty-four years. He taught us many things that are right: how to behave ourselves in appropriate ways, what it meant to be a person of integrity, and to respect the aged. I'm afraid I fell slightly short of that respect in disappointing him at the end when he could see my "white" hair—but even as he was dying, he managed to give me one more small, deep-throated chuckle about it, so I knew I was forgiven. Thank you for his life before me. I am forever grateful that You gave me to him to be my "Daddy. In Jesus' Name, Amen

"Hear, O my son, and receive my sayings; and the years of thy life shall be many." Proverbs 4:10

94. Mother

The following is a tribute I wrote for Mother's funeral. Tony Hall, the son of Bruce and Betty Hall, our faithful, loving, family friends for more than twenty-three years, read it.

Her flashing smile lit up every room she entered... Her laughter would fill your heart with sunshine just as the fruits from her garden would fill your belly with delicious meals.

The endless stories she told of her life growing up in Crandall, Texas, were entertaining and refreshing. A born-and-bred Texan, she never lost her love for the Lone Star State. Just this fall, she was asked what she wanted for Christmas. She replied, "To go to Crandall, just one more time."

She was a priceless mother and one who will always be missed but carried in the hearts of those who loved her. If each of her children were asked what they thought about their mother, they would reply:

Number one daughter, Sally Ann would say:

"We gained our love of reading from having Mother read so much to us as children. She read to us from the Hurlburt's Story of the Bible as we sat beside her every day. I often wondered why she never read anything but Edgar A. Guest, Reader's Digest, and Ideals Magazine for her own reading pleasure, and then it dawned on me that it was because she was too busy taking care of us and seeing to it that we read."

Number two daughter, Molly Lou would say:

"Mother was my very dearest and closest friend. She knew me, inside out and loved me anyway."

Number three daughter, Polly Pat would say:

"She never allowed us to whine, and always told us we could do and be anything we set our minds to be. She treated everyone the same way and was the same in private as she was in public. She hated hypocrisy."

Number four daughter, Ellen Sue would say:

"I was the last child born, and being number five, Mother had learned her job perfectly well and she did it."

Number one and only son, Bob, would say:

"Mother gave me my faith and taught me how to live. She always encouraged me and made me feel that I could do anything. She made me proud to be a Texan, and I have worn my Texas tie for her today."

Number six was Mother's friend for twenty-three years. Betty Hall was like a fifth daughter, and she would say of Mother:

"Polly was one of my dearest friends. We have prepared many meals together, spent hours visiting on the porch swing, and we were partners for hundreds of Forty-Two games. Polly always said she 'marked' our daughter, Angela with her laughing and talking, but really she left her mark on everyone she met with her zeal for life, her colorful stories, and her generosity. Honestly, she never met a stranger. She loved God, her family, her friends, and Texas. We will miss her fervently."

When we were growing up, we always heard Mother say, "All of my life I have been on the receiving end and my blessings just keep on coming. I don't understand why I have been so blessed."

We can answer that, Mother. You receive so much because you give so much. You always said that all you ever wanted for Christmas or any other occasion for a gift was for all five of your children to be Christians. "That," you said, "would be the best gift of all."

If you could speak to us now, Mother and you had to introduce us, here is what you would say in your poetic musical way, just as you always did: "These are our four daughters, my 'precious jewels', Sally Ann, Molly Lou, Polly Pat, and Ellen Sue. And this is our son, Bob, my 'pride and joy.'"

To you, Mother, we would say, "No one ever outgrows the need for a mother's love." We will always need and have your love to carry us through life until we meet again, hear your laughter, and see your sweet smile. Thank you for blessing our lives.

MAGNET MESSAGE:

My mother, Polly Rogers, passed from this life on January 16, 1997. She leaves behind a legacy of Christian living, cheer, and laughter. She was the sunshine in my soul and an example of a true Christian that anyone could be safe in following. I will miss her every day of my life.

"But as it is written, eye has not seen, nor ear heard, neither have entered into the heart of man, the things which God has prepared for those that love Him." I Corinthians 2:9

95. *The Most Thoughtful Gift*

"A ll it takes for a man to be happy is a good wife and a good pair of overalls."

These words of our father to us five children when we were small were truly what he believed.

A building contractor in the Oklahoma City area for almost thirty years, he literally lived in his overalls.

"Now Morris Rogers," Mother would say, "You wear those overalls everywhere, but you mustn't wear them to church!"

Daddy grinned. Such a thought surely never crossed his mind, as he "twinkled" in the light of Mother's knowing smile.

I don't remember Daddy ever leaving for work that he wasn't whistling, nor do I recall him ever coming home from work that he wasn't whistling.

"Morris, you act like you own the world," Mother commented one day as he came in whistling.

"My Father does," was his reply.

One night, Mother called us all to come into the living room. "I have an announcement to make," she told us.

We seated ourselves around her (my sister Sally Ann 13, me 11, and our brother Bob 7), eagerly waiting for what she was going to say.

"I'm that way," she said quietly. (Mother would never say

the word 'pregnant.')

"May I tell Daddy?" I asked excitedly.

"I think your father knows it."

Six months later, our sister, Polly Pat was born and Daddy even wore his overalls to the hospital!

Three years later, Mother again announced she was "that way" and our baby sister; Ellen Sue was born six months afterwards. And you guessed it! Daddy wore his overalls to the hospital that night, too.

When Mother died in 1997, Daddy was alone and without his mate of sixty-four years, and he found comfort in his beautiful garden. My favorite memory of him is seeing him in his garden, overalls on, and leaning on his hoe, wiping his brow with his shirtsleeve, hat in hand. He always said being in the garden was his "time with the Lord."

Not long after Mother's death, he fell and fractured his back. His eyesight almost completely gone, he opted to sell the house he had built in 1968 for Mother when he retired, and enter an assisted living facility. He was afraid of being a burden on his children.

Daddy loved to eat peanut butter straight out of the jar, and sometimes he didn't always see well enough to keep it off the bib of his overalls.

"Aw, Molly Lou, would you look at that? I can't seem to hit my mouth!" And he'd wipe "at" the spot on the front of his overalls, chuckling all the while.

The night Daddy died in 2002, and we had said our goodbyes to this, the dearest father on Earth, I left the residence without going back to his room. I knew that Polly Pat would

tend to cleaning it out and disposing of his overalls and shirts…. I thought!

The following Christmas, Polly Pat said she had a surprise for all four of her siblings. We all gathered at Ellen Sue's house and Polly Pat passed out the packages. I opened mine first. There before me was the most thoughtful gift I could ever receive!

I held in my hands a quilt made from Daddy's overalls! Polly Pat had made five of them, one for each of us!My quilt had the "bib," complete with peanut butter stains and I also had the little pocket, in which he kept his Bible that he wanted always with him to "…be ready always to give an answer to every man that asketh you a reason of the hope that is in you…" (I Peter 3:15).

As I lifted the quilt from its box, tears of sorrow, loneliness, joy, and healing all combined, poured onto my cheeks and spilled onto my sweater, as memories of Daddy swelled within my heart and soul.

From deep within, I could hear him say:

"All it takes for a man to be happy is a good wife and a good pair of overalls!"

Daddy had them both. And now I had the overalls!

Epilogue

I began this book in 1999, and it was published in 2000. It is very important to me to always recall the fond memories of days gone by. I would encourage everyone to grab pen and paper and begin TODAY to write your life's memories as you remember them. Don't worry about being historically accurate; just be emotionally accurate with your heart and mind as you recall the things that made you who you are today.

All of your life's experiences and adventures, whether good or bad, have gone into the making of your character. Those thoughts need to be put to the page for generations to read and learn to know you.

As you write, you will notice that one memory leads to another, and oftentimes, you will also notice that something you had long forgotten will surface. The image that returns to your mind may be a happy one, or it may be a sorrowful one. It doesn't matter; you need to record it. Happiness comes with writing if there are memories to share, and healing comes with writing if there are fences to mend. Either way, you are the recipient of the joy that follows. It's just an added "perk" to know that you have blessed others as well.

Be sure to put "heart" into all you write, for it is there that the healing, loving, and blessings begin.

And it is there that you will find a "peace that passes all understanding."

---Molly Lemmons c2007

About The Author

Molly Lemmons, an award-winning author and professional storyteller wrote a weekly column for the Mustang, Oklahoma news for over three years. When the newspaper changed management, she was asked by her readers to condense the columns into a book of the same name. Newspapers from Texas and Arkansas ran the column as well as Oklahoma and in 2000, her book, *Kind of Heart,* was published as a compilation of those columns.

Using heartwarming, humorous, inspirational, and exciting stories, this book bridges the gap between generations. She connects adult audiences to nearly forgotten values and experiences of the past, and introduces children to the common foibles and fun of life. Written from her heart, the reader will experience the nostalgia of days gone by.

Molly's stories have appeared in *Ideals Magazine, Chicken Soup for the Soul,* series of award-winning books, *Christian Woman,* and many other online publications. (*Heartcatchers,* and *Heartwarmers,* and *Write2the Heart.*)

Her other book, *The Passing of Paradise* was released for publication in 2005. The book, although classified as inspirational romance fiction is, nevertheless, a book based on true accounts of the lives of real people.

Retired from Mustang, OK public schools after 22 years, Molly spends her time in writing and traveling, telling her stories anywhere there is a need for stories that warm the heart and cause the listeners to celebrate God, life and families. She also teaches classes on "Writing and Telling Life's Memories" (from the heart) to book festivals and conferences around the state.

Molly Lemmons serves as secretary of the Oklahoma State Storytelling Organization, *The Territory Tellers;* she is a member of the *National Storytelling Network;* a member of *Oklahoma City Writers, Inc.; Oklahoma Writers Federation, Inc.;* and *Tejas Storytelling Association.*

An alumna of Oklahoma Christian University, she resides in Mustang, OK with her husband of 51 years, four cats and a Great Pyrenees dog. She is mother of two, and "Grand Molly" to two, Ric and Carly Meltabarger of Mustang, OK.

For information on availability for programs or classes, please contact her at mollyloubelle@cox.net and access her website for more information: http://mollyloubelle.com